BIG BOOK OF KNOWLEDGE

ADVERTISEMENT

Read a brighter future

The Week Junior is the award-winning, must-read magazine that inspires a love of reading and encourages kids to think for themselves.

Our expert editorial team packs thought-provoking facts and eye-catching images into every page. It inspires children to play a positive part in our world's future, to succeed in their futures — and to lead happy, fulfilling lives.

We all want to give our children the best start in life – an **open, enquiring mind** is the best gift you'll give them.

GET 6 FREE ISSUES AT
theweekjunior.co.uk/offer   Use code Y24BBOK

BIG BOOK OF KNOWLEDGE

BLOOMSBURY EDUCATION
LONDON OXFORD NEW YORK NEW DELHI SYDNEY

BLOOMSBURY EDUCATION

Bloomsbury Publishing Plc
50 Bedford Square, London, WC1B 3DP, UK
29 Earlsfort Terrace, Dublin 2, Ireland

BLOOMSBURY, BLOOMSBURY EDUCATION and the Diana logo are trademarks of Bloomsbury Publishing Plc

First published in Great Britain, 2024 by Bloomsbury Publishing Plc

This edition published in Great Britain, 2024 by Bloomsbury Publishing Plc

Text copyright © The Week Junior, Future Publishing Limited, 2024

The Week Junior, Future Publishing Limited have asserted their right under the Copyright, Designs and Patents Act, 1988, to be identified as Author of this work

Every reasonable effort has been made to trace and acknowledge copyright holders of material reproduced in this book, but if any have been inadvertently overlooked the publishers would be glad to hear from them. For legal purposes, the picture credits on p.240 constitute an extension of this copyright page.

All rights reserved. No part of this publication may be reproduced or transmitted in any form or by any means, electronic or mechanical, including photocopying, recording, or any information storage or retrieval system, without prior permission in writing from the publishers

A catalogue record for this book is available from the British Library

ISBN: HB: 978-1-8019-9522-1; ePDF: 978-1-8019-9523-8; ePub: 978-1-8019-9524-5

2 4 6 8 10 9 7 5 3 1 (hardback)

Text design by Peter Clayman, and Sophie Gordon

Printed and bound in China by Golden Prosperity Printing & Packaging (Huizhou) Co., Ltd., Guangdong, China

To find out more about our authors and books visit www.bloomsbury.com and sign up for our newsletters

CONTENTS

AMAZING ANIMALS 8

Animal achievements 10
Fuzzy feelings 12
Fuzzy friendships 14
... and fuzzy fun 16
Bird-brained? 18
Going wild 20
Mischief makers 22
Mutts on the move 24
Cat quests 28
Daring dashes 30

CREATURE FEATURES 32

Marvellous mammals 34
Remarkable reptiles 38
Amazing amphibians 42
Brilliant birds 46
Fantastic fish 50
Incredible insects 56

EARTH'S ENVIRONMENT 62

Good news stories 64
Humans harming the world 68
Beating the heat 72
Restoring balance 74
Making something from nothing . 76
Going green 78

PEOPLE POWER 86

Daredevils 88
Remarkable rescues 92
Fantastic finds 96

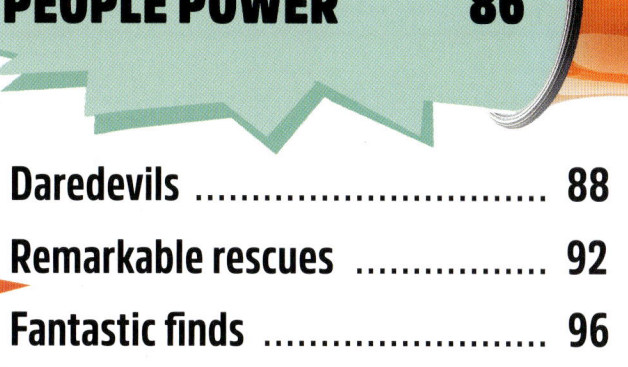

SENSATIONAL SCIENCE 100

Incredible AI 102
Switched on or silent? 106
Making ends meat 108
The proof's in the poo 110
Space: stranger than
science fiction 112

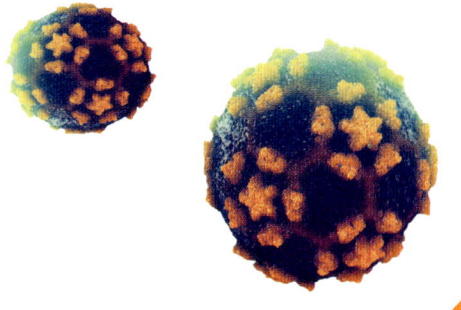

BRILLIANT BOOKS 116

Love your libraries 118
Ready to read? 122
Ready to write? 126

ASTONISHING ART 130

Arty food 132
... and foodie art 134
Cool canvases 136
Fake cake 140
Mystery models 142
Is it art? 144
Appreciating
astonishing art 146

FABULOUS FOOD 150

Super-sized 152
Nacho nibbles 154
Undercover vegetables 156
Fantastical flavours 158
A sweet and savoury salad 160

OUT AND ABOUT 162

Vacation creations 164
Terrible tourism 166
Odd jobs 168
What a way to live! 172
Funny festivals 174
High in the sky 176
Rare restaurants 178

SPECTACULAR SPORTS 180

Down and dirty 182
Fast and slow 184
Doubling up 186
Caught in the act 188
Spirited support 190
Finding your passion 192

WONDERFUL WELLBEING 198

Getting a great start 200
Succeeding at school 202
The foundations of friendship 204
Family time 206
Taking me time 208
Choose to snooze 210
Creating a self-care kit 212

STRANGE BUT TRUE 214

Days out for dust busters 216
Curious costumes 218
Mistaken for aliens 220
Colossal collections 222
How much? 226
Wooden wonders 228
Ridiculous wrongdoing 230

GLOSSARY 232
INDEX 236
IMAGE CREDITS 239

AMAZING ANIMALS

DON'T FORGET YOUR TRUNKS
Elephants are really good at swimming and can swim for up to six hours at a time.

ANIMAL ACHIEVEMENTS

Animals can be surprisingly artistic and amazingly athletic – just look at this talented trio.

Dogs perform with orchestra

Three new members of the Danish Chamber Orchestra unleashed their talents at a performance in 2023.

Before playing Leopold Mozart's *Hunting Symphony*, the orchestra introduced three paw-some soloists: dogs named Cookie, Sophus and Sica. Each talented pup had learned to bark or howl when the conductor gave special **cues**.

Cookie's owner said the pup "had a blast".

Athletic bird scoots to success

A cockatoo in Bulgaria has learned to impress audiences by riding a bird-sized scooter.

Chico rides by holding the handlebars in his beak while pushing off with his foot. The sporty bird can complete a five-metre course in under 15 seconds.

Chico can also pedal a tiny bicycle and dunk mini basketballs. "He is a natural talent," his owner said.

Painting pig amazes with artwork

Would you pay for a painting by a pig? One swine in South Africa creates works of art that have been sold for over £21,300.

The pig, who goes by the name "Pigcasso", was rescued by an animal shelter in 2016. The shelter's founder, Joanne Lefson, noticed that Pigcasso ate or destroyed just about everything in her path – except for some paintbrushes.

Lefson put a canvas in the pig's stall and encouraged her to paint. The 680-kilogram hog has now created more than 400 works of art.

Lefson believes that the painting pig's popularity is a sign of how amazing Pigcasso and other farm animals are. "You can't look at it and not place greater value on their intelligence … and creativity," she said.

FUZZY FEELINGS

Animals can also be amazingly affectionate. The way some creatures act around humans has made researchers curious to learn more about them.

Can meerkats read moods?

Scientists are trying to find out if meerkats can detect emotions in humans, such as happiness or anger.

The experts look at how the meerkats act around zookeepers and visitors, and check to see if the meerkats show **empathy**. The findings will be used to make meerkats more comfortable around humans, and could affect how meerkats' zoo homes are designed.

Horses hear human emotions

From *Black Beauty* to *The Chronicles of Narnia*, films and books have often shown the friendships that can develop between humans and horses. Lots of real-life stories confirm that horses seem to have a special understanding of humans.

However, until a study in 2023, nobody knew if horses really recognised different human emotions.

Researchers used a test that usually measures how much babies understand. One by one, 28 horses were shown a happy or sad human face. At the same time, a recording of a happy or sad voice was played.

The test showed that horses can match the two up. When the face and voice didn't match, the horses seemed to be puzzled. They looked at the picture for longer, as if they knew that something wasn't right.

The researchers still don't know if the horses understand what being sad or happy means. However, horses seem to prefer spending time around happy people because they spent longer looking at those pictures.

The researchers now want to see if horses can recognise other human emotions.

FUZZY FRIENDSHIPS...

Many species also seem to form friendships, and they have their own ways of showing them.

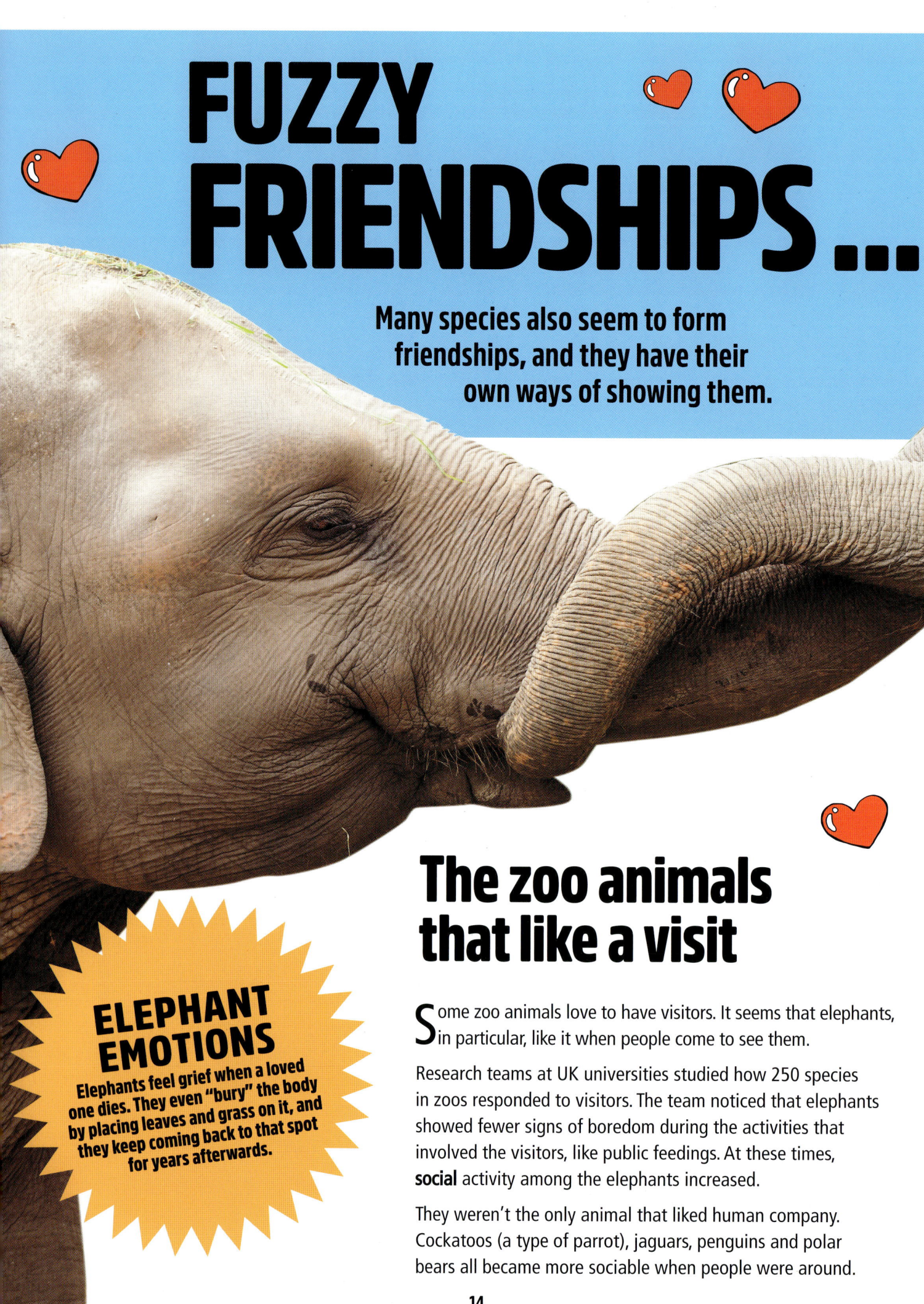

The zoo animals that like a visit

Some zoo animals love to have visitors. It seems that elephants, in particular, like it when people come to see them.

Research teams at UK universities studied how 250 species in zoos responded to visitors. The team noticed that elephants showed fewer signs of boredom during the activities that involved the visitors, like public feedings. At these times, **social** activity among the elephants increased.

They weren't the only animal that liked human company. Cockatoos (a type of parrot), jaguars, penguins and polar bears all became more sociable when people were around.

ELEPHANT EMOTIONS
Elephants feel grief when a loved one dies. They even "bury" the body by placing leaves and grass on it, and they keep coming back to that spot for years afterwards.

TEAMWORK

Dolphins have been seen working together to help each other and humans, apparently scaring off sharks.

FRIENDS IN NEED

Rats appear to care for their friends. One research team observed rats saving their friends from drowning and helping them to dry off.

They all lived happily ever after

The end of Gez Robinson's back garden in Yorkshire, UK, became like a Beatrix Potter story come to life. An unlikely friendship formed between a frog living in the garden pond and a nest of mice nearby. Robinson said, "People are amazed at the friendship."

Man saves crane and wins a friend

A man in India nursed a crane back to health after he found it with an injured foot on his farm. Gurjar expected the bird to fly away once it could stand on its own two feet, but it stayed.

Gurjar said, "On some days he flies away but always returns by sunset. Friendship **thrives** on freedom. He roams around freely and we never **constrain** him."

...AND FUZZY FUN

Love to laugh

Cows, foxes, apes, monkeys and seals are among dozens of animals that love to laugh.

Researchers in the US found that these creatures make "play **vocalisations**" as a way to invite other animals to join in their fun.

Some species, like rats, laugh at a pitch that is too high for humans to hear; others laugh loudly and clearly. Some laugh in a rhythmic pattern, and for others it's more of a short, sharp "ha!".

Types of laugh

Humans have lots of different ways to laugh too. At the University of Virginia, US, nearly 3,400 laughs were studied after people watched three types of videos.

Films that were funny in a normal, "straightforward" way led to a feel-good, catching kind of laughter.

Amusing videos that showed scenes that would be classed as "cute" produced quieter, shorter laughs.

Ones featuring things going wrong led to people guffawing more loudly and letting loose a sort of trumpet-like blast of laughter.

Have another look at the ways scientists found animals laugh – they seem to match up well.

That tickles!

At Humboldt University in Berlin, Germany, scientists tried a playful experiment with caged rats.

They tickled the rats on their tummies and backs, and let the rats chase the scientists' hands around the cage. Two rats were also seen chasing each other's tails and playfighting.

During the experiments, the rats' "giggling" was recorded using special microphones. Humans can't hear rat laughter because they squeak at a very high pitch – too high for our ears to pick up.

BIRD-BRAINED?

DID YOU KNOW? A group of magpies is called a "mischief".

The phrase "bird-brained" is often used to suggest a tiny brain – and a tiny amount of intelligence. We could learn a lot from magpies, though. These ones have even outsmarted the experts …

Scientists stumped

In 2022, A group of Australian magpies surprised scientists by spoiling their experiment. The scientists had fitted the birds with trackers in tiny backpack-like harnesses so they could study their behaviour.

However, other magpies pecked at the devices until the trackers fell off. Scientists say this shows magpies working together to solve problems. It suggests that the birds show concern for each other.

Birds stole anti-bird spikes

Dutch researchers discovered that birds living in cities are stealing the metal spikes that humans put on buildings to keep them away – and using them to protect their nests.

Auke-Florian Hiemstra, a Dutch nest expert, found an enormous magpie nest made from around 1,500 metal spikes, all pointing outwards to ward off **predators**.

Researchers then found that 50 metres of anti-bird spikes that had been glued to a nearby hospital's roof had been ripped out – presumably by the magpies.

Hiemstra told the BBC that he was amazed by the "strange, beautiful, weird nest".

Magpies are known for using thorny branches to protect their nests. However, humans tend to dig up or chop down prickly plants in cities.

In the past, the birds have been known to use telephone wires, knitting needles, clothes hangers and barbed wire. The researchers say that this is the first time birds have been observed using humans' anti-bird devices against them.

Hiemstra and the magpie nest.

Smart seagulls

Fed up with gulls stealing your food? Try hiding when you eat it. Scientists have found that gulls are far more likely to eat something if they see humans eating it first.

Need any help with those chips?

GOING WILD

We know that animals can be talented, friendly, funny, cute and clever – but they can also be pests. These curious creatures simply chewed up the rule book.

Bear breaks into bakery

A bear in Italy raided a bakery for biscuits.

The bear, known as Juan Carrito, broke into Marina Valentini's bakery, Dolci Momenti (which means "sweet moments"). The bear smashed the window and helped himself to a handful of sweet treats.

"He must have smelled them wafting down the street," said Valentini. She noted that tourists often came in asking, "Are these the biscuits the bear ate?"

Did someone say biscuits?

Badger gives chase

A badger caused chaos in a petrol station by chasing a customer around the shop.

Molly Padget stopped at the garage in Stafford, UK, to fill up with petrol and buy some dinner. The badger chased her down two aisles, causing her to drop her curry in shock.

The badger didn't go in to shop, however. "He didn't take anything; he just ran into the loos," Molly said.

Another customer asked staff for a broom and used it to guide the badger back outside. It then hurried off home.

Pet duck runs amok

A pet duck named Ham became an online sensation after his owner started sharing his mischievous behaviour on social media.

Ham kept escaping from his pen, chasing foxes and waddling into other people's houses. At home, the **domesticated** duck's favourite snack was a bowl of Rice Krispies® and a cup of tea.

MISCHIEF MAKERS

Renegade otter steals surfboards

A **renegade** sea otter terrorised the California coast.

The thieving critter, a five-year-old female known to authorities as Otter 841, climbed onto people's surfboards and sank her teeth into them.

One teen surfer let go of his board and watched as 841 commandeered it. "The otter was **shredding**, caught a couple of nice waves," he said.

Bold bird divides English village

Oi, this is MY village.

A jackdaw nicknamed Derek was a common sight for people living in the village of Rossington, UK.

Not everybody liked the bird, though. Derek seemed to delight in dive-bombing children as they played outdoors – leaving them "**petrified**" to go outside.

Although some villagers wanted him locked up, others said that the bird was simply looking for company. He was even spotted sitting on schoolchildren's shoulders.

"He just wants to be your friend," said one resident.

Two cheeky emus come home

A pair of emus that were "banned" from a hotel in the town of Yaraka, Australia, insisted on returning.

The cheeky emus, called Kevin and Carol, had been straying into the hotel, snatching toast from guests, drinking tourists' tea and making a mess with their poo.

After disappearing for nearly three years, the pair were spotted again – with emu chicks. The birds spent most of the time with their chicks, but local resident Leanne Byrne said that Carol sometimes stopped by for a cuddle.

MUTTS
ON THE MOVE

None of these dogs has followed a command to "Stay!". Can you guess which had help getting home and which took matters into their own paws? Find out the answers over the page.

The great escapes

1: Bluebell's minibreak

Imagine being given the wrong dog. That's what happened to the Miller family when they returned to their home in Nashville, US, from the UK.

Meanwhile, Bluebell – their actual pet dog – had been put on the wrong flight and ended up more than 11,250 kilometres away in Riyadh, Saudi Arabia.

Did Bluebell manage to sniff her way onto a flight that smelled more like home?

2: Runaway Ralph

A dog gave his owner a scare when he decided to bolt off from his morning walk and try travelling from Wrexham in Wales to Manchester Airport in the UK.

The three-year-old pooch, named Ralph, clearly fancied going on holiday. With his owner distracted, Ralph hopped into a taxi with a family who was on their way to the airport.

Did he hop back out or get to the airport?

3: Bolting Bailey

A Texas family was worried when their dog Bailey, a husky mix they had recently adopted, got spooked and ran away from home.

They contacted the Animal Rescue League of El Paso, a shelter that had previously cared for Bailey, to tell the staff that she was missing.

Did the rescue centre send out a search party or did Bailey bring herself back?

4: Pepper pads off

After getting lost in a park in Hertfordshire, UK, a dog called Pepper was last seen heading towards a busy town centre. However, it was over three kilometres away.

Did Pepper make it to town or find a friend on the way?

The real returns

1: Bluebell's minibreak

Bluebell required help and it had to be extreme.

The Millers needed to take three flights to reach Saudi Arabia and bring their beloved pet home.

2: Runaway Ralph

Ralph was taken – but then returned. There was no phone number on the dog's collar and the family didn't want to miss their flight. They decided simply to take him with them to the airport.

Thankfully, the airport staff helped. Ralph and his owner were finally reunited.

3: Bolting Bailey

Bailey found her way back alone, but to the shelter rather than to her new home.

She walked about 16 kilometres and then, three days after bolting off, showed up at the shelter. She quickly made her presence known – in an unexpected way.

"I'll be darn," said shelter founder Loretta Hyde. "At 1:42 in the morning she's ringing the doorbell."

"These dogs are smarter than people give them credit for," she said.

In the morning, Bailey was reunited with her owners. She's now enjoying her new home.

4: Pepper pads off

Pepper needed no help at all. She trotted straight to the town centre bus station, hopped on the No.7 (the right bus to take her home) and took a seat. The clever canine is a border collie: a breed known for being very intelligent.

A woman on the bus recognised Pepper and phoned the owners. When the bus got near the dog's stop, the woman reported, "She got up, the doors opened and she jumped off." The woman then waited with Pepper.

Pepper's owners, Charlotte Jones and Saffron Caps, couldn't believe it. A very relieved and proud Jones said, "It was like something out of *Lassie*."

CAT QUESTS

Think cats are too fond of their creature comforts? Think again. Dogs aren't the only pets who break away for adventure.

A pet gets packed up

Security officials at New York City's John F. Kennedy airport, US, spotted an unusual shape while scanning a man's luggage. A tuft of orange fur poking out from the black bag led to the discovery that a family member's cat had curled up inside the suitcase.

The feline was safely returned home and the man later booked a new, cat-free flight to his destination.

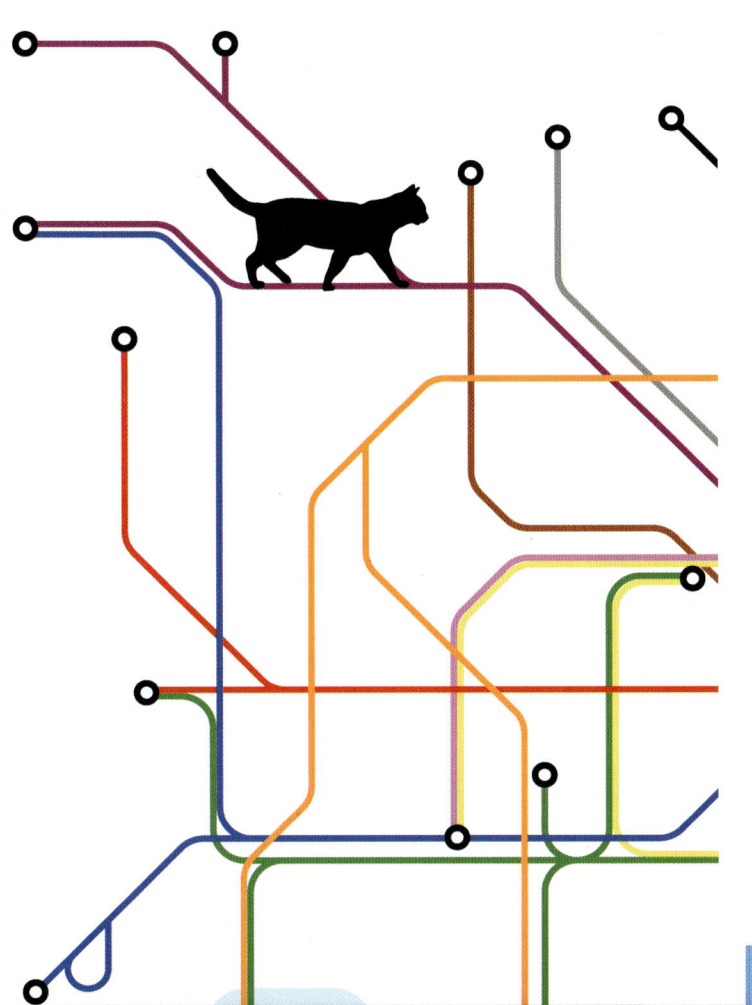

Surprise in the underground

A cat that spent two weeks inside the London Underground subway system was found dusty but safe. Station staff heard him meowing in the tunnels and saw him looking for food on the platform at night.

Station manager David Nobbs said, "I've been working on the London Underground for 16 years and you get all walks of life coming through, but never before a cat on the loose."

Some people think the cat, Mr Jingles, was trying to spot his train home.

A curious cat travels the world

A rescue cat called Bao Zi has been busy travelling around the world with her owners, Hélène and Alice. The couple love freedom, being **spontaneous** and seeing new places, and they wanted their cat to go with them.

The travelling trio has visited 22 national parks, five countries and 45 US states.

DARING DASHES

It's not just precious pets who break free ...

Adventurous animal takes a stroll

A curious red panda took the chance to enjoy a spot of sightseeing in the town of Newquay, UK, after she escaped from the local zoo.

The animal, named Sundara, was seen by staff working at a **greengrocer's** shop about half a mile from Newquay Zoo. A juicy apple was rolled towards her to keep her busy until help arrived.

DID YOU KNOW? Red pandas are more closely related to skunks, weasels and raccoons than they are to giant pandas.

A most colourful escape

Police in Pennsylvania, US, chased down an unusual runaway: a peacock passenger.

The **culprit** was a pet peacock named Blue, who had climbed onto the top of his owner's van and hitched a ride out of town.

Blue led officers on a daring chase through a local neighbourhood before being reunited with his owner, safe and unharmed.

Home sssweet home

A two-metre-long king cobra named Sir Vass escaped from his **enclosure** in a Swedish zoo – but didn't get far. He simply hid inside the walls.

After a week, though, life on the run was "too stressful", a museum official said. Sir Vass slithered back home without anyone interfering.

Real OR rubbish?
A very slow escape artist

Tank the tortoise succeeded in escaping from a vet's office in Pennsylvania, US – three times. "He just decided he was going to high-tail it and go on an adventure," said vet Megan McFarland. She asked locals to look out for "a large boulder eating in your garden" but not to be alarmed because "he's actually very sweet". On his third escape, the wily tortoise travelled about two miles before he was found.

Is this story real or is it artifi-shell?*

***Real!** The vets decided to put a GPS tracker on Tank so that he can be found quickly if he escapes yet again.

CREATURE

FEATURES

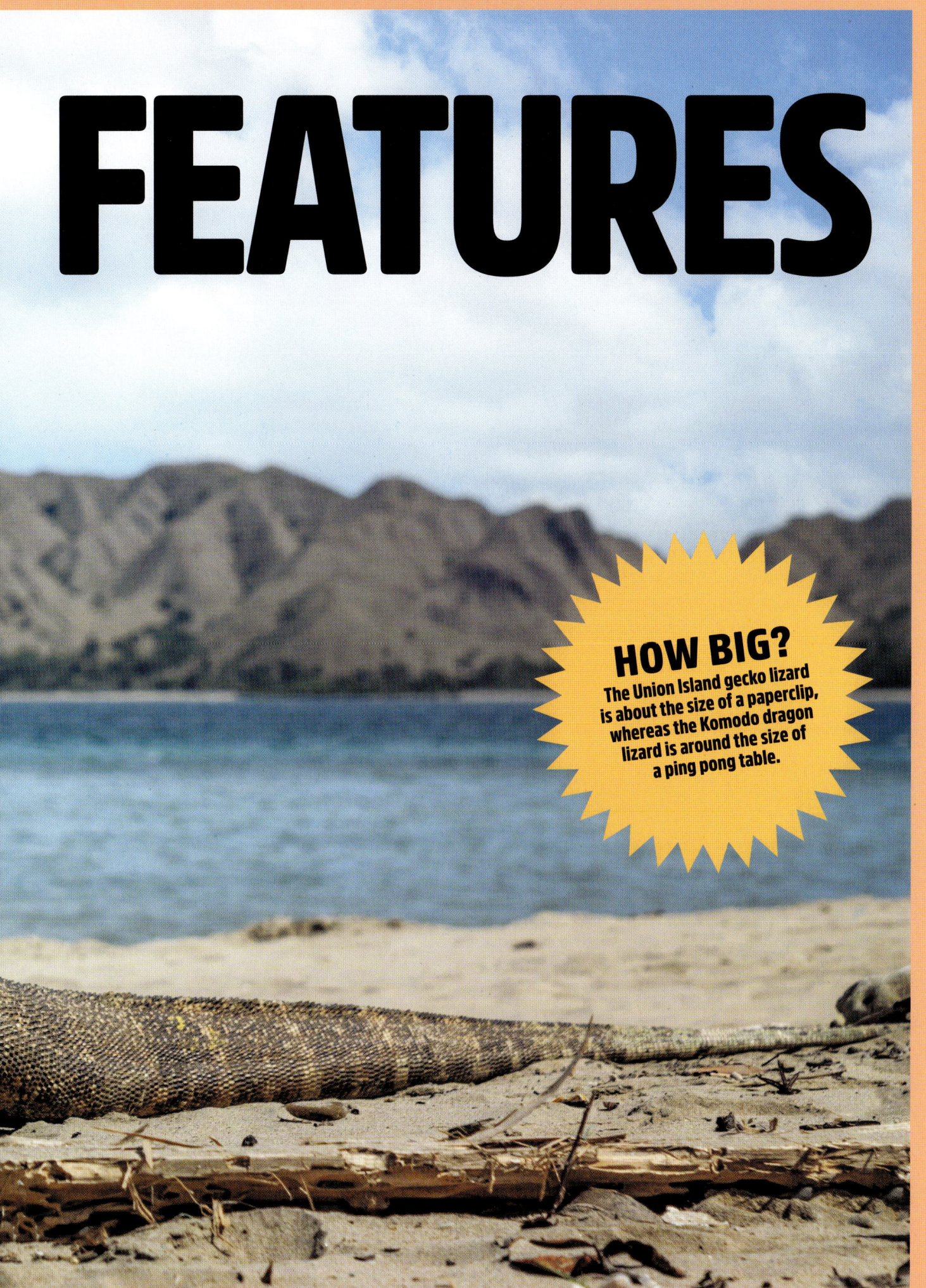

HOW BIG?
The Union Island gecko lizard is about the size of a paperclip, whereas the Komodo dragon lizard is around the size of a ping pong table.

MARVELLOUS MAMMALS

DID YOU KNOW? Humans are mammals.

Animal identifier: mammals		
Bones:	Yes	✓
	No	
Skin:	Hairy	✓
	Smooth	
	Scaly	
	Feathery	
Breathing:	In water	
	In air	✓
Blood:	Cold	
	Warm	✓
Babies:	Live, without shells	✓
	From hard-shelled eggs	
	From soft-shelled eggs	

Gibbons plan their breakfast

Would you get up earlier in the morning if you knew you could have your favourite breakfast? A study has found that Skywalker gibbons do just that when they fancy fruit.

Gibbons eat a mixture of fruit and tree leaves. Researchers found that when they ate fruit for breakfast, they left their sleeping trees up to an hour earlier. This may be because other animals also eat fruit for breakfast and so there is a lot of competition to be the first to get to the fruit trees.

The team also found that gibbons set off later when they slept in large groups – because they couldn't agree on a place to go for breakfast.

The tiniest bats

The pipistrelle bat is the smallest kind living in the UK, weighing about seven grams – the same as a 2p coin – with a wingspan of 20 centimetres.

However, that looks enormous compared to the Kitti's hog-nosed bat, also known as the bumblebee bat, which is found in Thailand and Myanmar. It weighs just two grams, and its wingspan can be as small as 13 centimetres.

The pipistrelle bat.

Red squirrels get pine marten guards

Pine martens are one of the UK's rarest meat-eating mammals. Their population has got smaller because of hunting and loss of natural habitats. However, they may now have a new role.

Pine martens in Scotland are being encouraged into habitats where they can protect red squirrels from greys.

Grey squirrels were introduced to the UK in the 1800s and have spread rapidly. They eat food needed by **native** UK red squirrels, and spread a disease that affects only reds.

Researchers have found that pine martens like to hunt large grey squirrels far more than speedy red ones. A bigger population of pine martens could stop greys from heading into red squirrels' habitats.

Don't pet these cats!

Animal **psychologists** asked zookeepers to answer questions on Amur tigers' behaviour. They observed two distinct personality types: one proud and dignified and the other steady and gentle. Proud tigers seemed to have more power; steady ones had closer relationships. Male and female tigers fell into both categories.

CANINES
Domestic dogs, foxes, wolves and other wild dogs are called "canines".

FELINES
Domestic cats, lions, tigers and other wild cats are called "felines".

Don't pet these dogs!

Researchers studied differences between UK country foxes and city foxes by giving them "puzzle feeders": they needed to solve puzzles to get the food inside. Although both types could solve the puzzles eventually, city foxes were bolder. Foxes from London did best – possibly because they're most used to competition and challenges.

Spotlight: Whales

Learning how to speak to whales

A team of scientists say that they could be one step closer to learning how to speak to whales.

Whales communicate by using a series of clicks, which the scientists examined for patterns using **AI** (artificial intelligence). The scientists then tried to match the sound patterns with the whales' behaviour.

The scientists think that they've translated their first word: "dive".

Why whales wear seaweed

Many different species of whale have been filmed playing with seaweed or wearing it like a hat; it's known as "kelping" (as kelp is a type of seaweed).

Researchers have discovered that kelping might be a useful way for whales to scratch an itch and get rid of pesky **parasites** such as whale lice.

The researchers also noticed that the whales appear to be doing it by choice, and don't seem stressed or hungry – so they may simply find it fun.

DID YOU KNOW?
There are around 90 different species of whale around the world.

Monster myths based on reality

Ancient **myths** about sea monsters could have been **inspired** by real-life whales that were using an unusual feeding method that scientists recorded for the first time in 2011. The whales point their bodies upright in the sea, mouths wide open, waiting for fish to swim straight in.

This method of eating looks a bit like pictures of ancient sea monsters, a similarity spotted by Dr John McCarthy from Flinders University, Australia.

He learned about a sea monster that **Vikings** called the "hafgufa", and a similar creature called an "aspidochelone" that appears in ancient Greek stories from nearly 2,000 years ago.

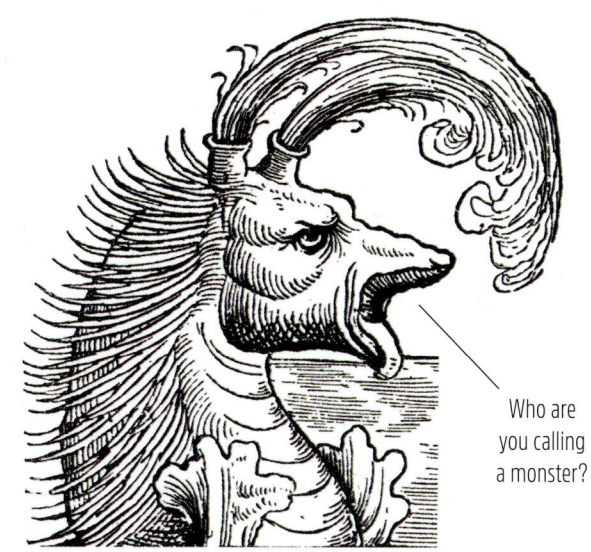

Who are you calling a monster?

Both monsters would open their mouths wide above the surface of the sea and wait for fish to leap in, wafting a "good smelling odour" from their mouths to attract the fish.

REMARKABLE REPTILES

Snaps, whooshes and moos

In 2023, experts used technology to study the calls of West African dwarf crocodiles.

The animals make some strange noises, some of them a bit like a howling wind and others like a mooing cow. The human ear often can't pick up these sounds, so the study will help experts to monitor the crocodiles in the wild.

Animal identifier: reptiles

Bones:	Yes	✓
	No	☐
Skin:	Hairy	☐
	Smooth	☐
	Scaly	✓
	Feathery	☐
Breathing:	In water	☐
	In air	✓
Blood:	Cold	✓
	Warm	☐
Babies:	Live, without shells	☐
	From hard-shelled eggs	✓
	From soft-shelled eggs	☐

DID YOU KNOW?
If an animal has cold blood, its surroundings control its temperature. To stay warm, it needs to be somewhere warm: it can't create its own heat.

Therapy lizard calms visitors

Taz isn't a typical lizard. Rather than spending his days sunning himself and snacking on flies, he is a therapy lizard for a charity called Disability Support in Nottingham, UK.

Staff noticed that the black-and-white tegu lizard seems to have a calming effect on people who visit the organisation's community centre.

Charlotte Throssel, the centre's manager, said, "When they get their courage up to stroke him, you can see everything just slow and relax instantly."

Tortoise approaches 200

A giant tortoise called Jonathan is thought to be approaching his 200th birthday. Nobody can be sure exactly how old he is, but a photo taken in 1882 shows that he was already fully grown then. Scientists used the picture to try to determine his age, and in 2022 he was estimated to be 190 years old.

Spotlight: Snakes

ASK AN EXPERT

How do snakes unhinge their jaw?

Snakes' heads are made up of many small bones. Some of these bones, like the ones protecting the brain, are joined together and don't move. Others have a joint allowing them to move a great deal.

Snakes do not have a chin like we do; instead, the two halves of the lower jaw are joined by a stretchy **ligament**. This allows them to separate far apart and for the snake's mouth to fit around its **prey**, even if the prey is wider than the snake's own head.

A snake's unhinged jaw allows it to eat whole eggs.

The spinning serpent

Scientists have discovered that dwarf reed snakes don't just slither away to avoid being captured by predators – they cartwheel. The snake curls its body into an S-shape before using its tail to launch into the air and do a cartwheel.

FACT FOCUS

An asssssstonishing size

The longest Burmese python ever recorded was caught in Florida, US. It was 5.8 metres long, which is as long as an adult giraffe is tall.

Burmese pythons don't have very good eyesight, so they sense prey using chemical receptors in their tongues and heat sensors along their jaws.

DID YOU KNOW? There are more than 4,000 different species of snake around the world.

Reptile gets a famous name

A species of snake discovered in Peru was given the Latin name *Tachymenoides harrisonfordi* after the actor Harrison Ford.

Ford seems to be surprised by this.

"These scientists keep naming critters after me, but it's always the ones that terrify children," Ford said. "I don't understand. I spend my free time cross-stitching. I sing lullabies to my basil plants."

AMAZING AMPHIBIANS

Animal identifier: amphibians		
Bones:	Yes	✓
	No	☐
Skin:	Hairy	☐
	Smooth	✓
	Scaly	☐
	Feathery	☐
Breathing:	In water	✓
	In air	✓
Blood:	Cold	✓
	Warm	☐
Babies:	Live, without shells	☐
	From hard-shelled eggs	☐
	From soft-shelled eggs	✓

Great crested newts saved by dogs

Great crested newts are rare, and it's illegal to harm them or their habitat.

To make sure that they were doing the right thing, a building company in Warrington, UK, came up with a creative way to find out whether the creatures were on possible building sites: they used sniffer dogs. These dogs hunted out the newts without hurting them.

Humans help toads cross the road

Drivers in the UK don't need to be "toad" twice to watch out for amphibians on the road.

Every spring, toads leave their winter **hibernation** hideouts and travel to breed at the ponds where they were born. For more than three weeks, over 400 metres of a road in south-west London, UK, is closed to allow them to cross.

Residents say that they're not bothered by the detour. "Toad patrol" volunteers help to redirect drivers and save the creatures from falling into drains.

The hopper that's a whopper

A giant toad weighing 2.7 kilograms was found in Conway National Park in Queensland, Australia. The enormous amphibian is thought to be the largest cane toad ever found.

Ranger Kylee Gray spotted the toad, describing it as "like a football with legs". She believed that it had probably been gorging on a diet of endless insects, reptiles and small mammals such as mice.

"A cane toad that size will eat anything it can fit into its mouth," she said. The toad has since been given the nickname "Toadzilla".

DID YOU KNOW?
Unlike mammals and reptiles, amphibians cannot chew their food and instead swallow their prey whole.

FACT FOCUS: Run, don't hop

The natterjack toad, an **endangered** species in the UK, has an unusual way of getting around. Instead of hopping like other frogs and toads, it runs around on its four legs.

Spotlight: Frogs

Frogs that pretend to be poo

Wallace's flying frogs have a particularly off-putting disguise from predators: they seem to pretend that they're poo.

When they're young, Wallace's flying frogs have reddish-brown bodies covered in small white dots. This appears like poo to birds above them.

Researchers in Austria tested out how effective the disguise is: they displayed models of the frogs with and without the spots to predator birds. The models with white spots attracted far less attention.

Disguising themselves as poo isn't the only way that these amphibians avoid becoming lunch. They can leap between branches and stretch out their webbed feet, which can help them to glide up to 16 metres.

DID YOU KNOW? There are more than 7,500 different species of frog around the world.

An adult Wallace's flying frog leaping between branches.

A pair of transparent frogs

In 2022, two new species of see-through frog were identified in Ecuador, South America. See-through frogs, known as glass frogs, have completely transparent skin. This means their insides can be seen.

At first, scientists thought that these two frogs – which were found at different ends of the same river – were from the same species. However, when they **analysed** the frogs' **DNA**, they found important differences. The frogs also made different sounds.

Although they've only just been identified, both species are considered endangered because of threats to their habitat.

A glass frog

Real OR rubbish?

Frogs and French villagers live in harmony

Residents of Frontenex village in France are woken each night by the song of three loud frogs. The froggy choir lives in Colette Ferry's garden pond, where neighbours often gather for the frogs' beautiful night-time concert.

Is this story real or are we ribbetting rubbish?*

***Rubbish!** Frontenex residents were constantly woken by frogs, but found them so annoying that they reported them to the police.

BRILLIANT BIRDS

Animal identifier: birds		
Bones:	Yes	☑
	No	☐
Skin:	Hairy	☐
	Smooth	☐
	Scaly	☑
	Feathery	☑
Breathing:	In water	☐
	In air	☑
Blood:	Cold	☐
	Warm	☑
Babies:	Live, without shells	☐
	From hard-shelled eggs	☑
	From soft-shelled eggs	☐

ASK AN EXPERT

Why are penguins black and white?

This is a clever form of camouflage that is known as countershading. It helps species, including penguins, to blend into their surroundings and avoid predators.

For example, if a hungry shark or orca was looking down, a penguin's black back would blend into the dark depths of the ocean. If they were looking up, a penguin's white belly would blend into the light of the sky above.

A hawk with an important job

Although Rufus the bird may look like an ordinary Harris's hawk, he has a very important job at one of the world's biggest tennis competitions. In 2022, he completed his 15th year of service as an official pest controller, scaring pigeons away from the Wimbledon tennis courts.

Handler Donna Davis said that Rufus seems "quite happy" to arrive early in the morning and fly around the courts, watching for pigeons that might disrupt games or poo on visitors.

DID YOU KNOW? Birds have scaly legs and feet.

A very emu-tional journey

An emu named Erasmo was looking for love in all the wrong places when he escaped from home. Erasmo, a flightless bird, climbed over a fence into the backyard of a private clinic that had a disc golf net.

Erasmo's owner joked that the net looked sort of like a female emu – "if you squint your eyes".

Police were called with a report of a "loose emu in the area", and Erasmo was safely returned home.

"Emus are great," Erasmo's owner said. "They're so sheepish and awkward. I'm kind of surprised more people don't have them."

I'm in love.

Spotlight: Parrots

DID YOU KNOW?
There are around 400 species of parrot across the world.

Can parrots really talk?

Parrots can **mimic** each other's calls, other birds and humans. They do this to communicate and create long-lasting friendships.

Parrots have a syrinx, similar to our vocal cords, which they vibrate with air from their lungs to create a sound. When they are "talking", parrots are mimicking people. However, some parrots seem to understand what a human is saying. They respond with a reply that they have learned.

No contest for the kakapo

The 2022 Bird of the Year competition in New Zealand made headline news after the kakapo, the world's heaviest species of parrot, was banned from the contest.

The kakapo is the only species to be voted New Zealand's favourite bird in two separate years, 2008 and 2020. However, organisers of the contest kept the species out so that voters would consider other birds that may have been overlooked.

"If the same bird keeps winning every year, that might make it not so interesting," an organiser said.

Reactions were mixed. "The right decision," one person said.

"He was robbed," said another.

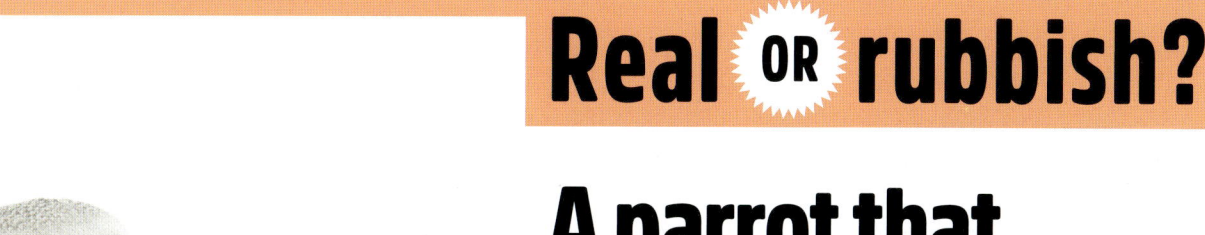

Real or rubbish?

A parrot that paints pictures

Scientists have discovered an African grey parrot with artistic talent. The parrot, named Echo, was spotted in the wild in East Africa. She was crushing berries with her beak and then using sticks to paint the juice onto rocks.

Echo was taken to the Maryland Zoo, US, where keepers provided paints and canvases to their new artist-in-residence.

Is this a true story or are we winging it?*

*__Rubbish!__ Echo does make art, but she was not discovered with the skill in the wild. The Maryland Zoo is teaching her to paint using paint-dipped sponges.

FANTASTIC FISH

Animal identifier: fish

Bones:	Yes	☑
	No	☐
Skin:	Hairy	☐
	Smooth	☐
	Scaly	☑
	Feathery	☐
Breathing:	In water	☑
	In air	☐
Blood:	Cold	☑
	Warm	☐
Babies:	Live, without shells	☐
	From hard-shelled eggs	☐
	From soft-shelled eggs	☑

SNEAKY
Trumpetfish are very slim. They can sneak up on prey by swimming carefully upright

trumpetfish

parrotfish

Undercover fish hides so it can hunt

Trumpetfish have discovered the ultimate disguise to sneak up on their prey: they hide behind bigger, non-threatening fish, like parrotfish.

A team of researchers decided to test if the method worked. They moved model trumpetfish and parrotfish through several groups of damselfish, a species commonly eaten by trumpetfish.

When the trumpetfish model moved past, the damselfish swam away very quickly. When a model parrotfish moved past, they didn't react in the same way. Then the researchers attached the models together. The damselfish reacted in the same way as they did when they saw just the parrotfish and not the trumpetfish.

So their sneaky method worked.

damselfish

A goldfish giant

Goldfish are normally small enough to live in tanks in people's homes. However, one enormous example proves the huge effect that **cross-breeding** can have.

The world's biggest goldfish, nicknamed "The Carrot", is half goldfish and half carp (a fish usually caught as food). It weighs a whopping 30 kilograms, which is around as much as a 10-year-old child.

Shocking dance moves

The elephant-nosed fish may look funny, but it has shocking powers. It can produce a small electrical field around itself, which it uses to detect when prey and underwater obstacles are nearby.

In 2023, researchers discovered that it also does a strange kind of dance to identify objects. The movements allow the fish to build up an electric image that helps it to "see".

Spotlight: Sharks

Whale sharks get tidy-ups

Whale sharks in Australia have learned that swimming up to scientists means that they get a nice body scrub.

Researchers have spent years scraping parasites off whale sharks, in order to understand more about the world's biggest fish. However, scientists have recently noticed that the sharks have started to slow down – and sometimes even stop swimming – as they approach, making it easier for the research divers to scrape off parasites.

It shows that the sharks remember that they feel better after a clean. It's also thought that they might be able to swim better when free of parasites.

FACT FOCUS: Stressed sharks

Some **tourists** pay to swim with sharks, but the sharks may not enjoy it. Researchers saw them move in quick zigzags alongside people, which is how they move when they're avoiding predators.

DID YOU KNOW? There are around 126 different species of shark around the world.

A scalloped hammerhead shark

The sharks that hold their breath

Scalloped hammerhead sharks hold their breath to keep their bodies warm while they're diving into cold water.

These sharks do deep dives into extremely cold water at night. However, researchers found that their body temperatures didn't drop until they started to return to the surface of the water. The scientists think they might be able to explain why.

Like most fish, sharks get their oxygen from water, which washes through their **gills** so that blood vessels can absorb oxygen from the water. This is where sharks are most likely to lose heat.

The experts believe that if the deep-diving sharks didn't get cold, they must have closed their gills. In other words, they were holding their breath as they dived. The research team called it a "complete surprise".

Other undersea swimmers

Fish share the seas with some truly amazing animals.

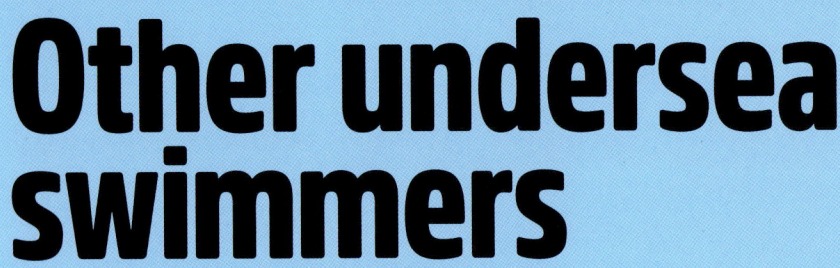

Octopuses have a mini brain in each arm.

Octopuses might have dreams

Scientists may have caught video footage of an octopus having dreams.

Researchers began watching videos of a sleeping Brazilian reef octopus called Costello, after noticing ink in his water tank one morning.

Over a month, the team saw four instances of Costello acting as if he were being attacked while he slept. The octopus flailed his **tentacles**, tried to make himself look bigger and shot out jets of ink.

"It was really bizarre because it looked like he was in pain," researcher Eric Angel Ramos said. "And then he just got up like nothing had happened."

The researchers think that this behaviour could have been triggered by a nightmare, resulting from Costello's experience of losing a tentacle to a predator earlier in life – but they can't be sure.

"There's still so much we don't know," Ramos said.

A vibrant shoreline surprise

A woman searching for wildlife along a UK seashore came across a colourful surprise. After picking up a large rock, Vicky Barlow said, "Something extremely bright and unusual caught my eye."

It was a rainbow sea slug: a rare **mollusc** typically found in warmer waters. Barlow said that she watched "in complete awe" as the sea slug uncurled and began exploring.

"It had quite the personality," she said.

ASK AN EXPERT

What kinds of jellyfish glow?

Many species of jellyfish, including the crystal jelly and crown jellies, can produce their own light using a process called bioluminescence. They use this light to attract prey.

Many of these bioluminescent jellies live in the deep ocean, which is reached by very little to no light.

INCREDIBLE INSECTS

Bumblebees like to play

Given a choice between food and playing, bees often choose to play first. Bumblebees in one study were given the options of a sweet snack and small wooden balls to roll. They rolled the balls up to 117 times, even though the sugary treat was nearby.

Animal identifier: birds		
Bones:	Yes	☑
	No	☐
Skin:	Hairy	☐
	Smooth	☐
	Scaly	☑
	Feathery	☑
Breathing:	In water	☐
	In air	☑
Blood:	Cold	☐
	Warm	☑
Babies:	Live, without shells	☐
	From hard-shelled eggs	☑
	From soft-shelled eggs	☐

Moths are super pollinators

A lot of attention is drawn to bees as super **pollinators**, and efforts to protect and encourage them have been growing. However, moths are just as important.

A study has shown that moths carry more pollen than bees and visit lots of different plants, some of which bees would not visit. Experts believe that this suggests moths could be responsible for a third of all the pollination of flowering plants in towns and cities.

The number of moths in the UK has fallen dramatically over the past 50 years. Dr Emilie Ellis, who worked on the study, said that it's important to make sure that green areas are attractive to moths as well as to bees.

Wasps seek out sweet things

Wasps are not very popular, despite killing pests and pollinating flowers. You might have more sympathy for them if you knew their situation at the end of the summer.

An adult wasp's job is to feed wasp **larvae** with insects. In return, the larvae produce a sugary treat for them. However, at the end of summer, wasp nest leaders stop laying eggs, so wasps lose their sugar supply.

That's why they prey on our picnics — when summer ends they're even hungrier than the picnicking people.

EXOSKELETONS
Insects have **exoskeletons** instead of bones. Beetles have very hard, smooth exoskeletons. Flies have softer, hairy ones. Moths' and butterflies' exoskeletons have tiny scales.

Spotlight: Ants

Ants use landmarks to get home

Researchers have found that ants build tall structures outside their nests to help them to find their way home.

Scientists studied ants living on **salt pans**. These ants travel long distances to find food. However, if the landscape doesn't vary, it can be hard for them to find their way back.

Ants from nests near features like shrubs build tiny mounds. In contrast, ants with nests in wide unchanging areas build mounds up to 40 centimetres high to guide them home.

FACT FOCUS: Speedy critters

The world's fastest ant takes nearly 50 strides per second. The Saharan silver ant barely lets its feet touch the ground as it runs.

Ants could help to sniff out disease

Doctors could have an unexpected new animal assistant in the fight against disease. A team of French scientists showed that ants are surprisingly good at sniffing out cancer.

Despite their tiny size, a common species of black ant has **evolved** a great sense of smell to sniff out food. Ants are also speedy learners with good memories, quickly remembering a smell if it's associated with a sugary reward.

The scientists trained ants to link the smell of lab-grown cancer cells with food. After just 30 minutes of training, the ants would sniff out cancer cells and could even tell the difference between types of the disease.

ASK AN EXPERT

How are ants so strong?

Ants are strong because of the shape of their bodies, which are perfectly adapted to carrying things larger than them.

They might have small bodies but they have strong jaws for gripping objects and sticky feet that stop them from overbalancing. This allows them to carry things that are up to 100 times their body weight.

DID YOU KNOW?
There are more than 15,700 different species of ant around the world.

Other curious creepy-crawlies

These tiny creatures aren't insects, but they're still marvellous minibeasts.

Not-so-scary spiders

Fear of spiders exists all over the world. People call this fear "arachnophobia". The word part "arachno" refers to spiders. The meaning of "phobia" is interesting – it actually means an overwhelming fear that's irrational: it might not have a sensible reason.

There are lots of reasons to be fond of spiders. They're fascinating: in fact, they're among the earliest land-living animals to exist, having evolved around 345 million years ago.

Every year, the world's spiders chomp through up to 800 million tonnes of prey, such as insects. This helps protect crops and other plant life.

The silk that they spin into webs is extraordinary. As well as being only sticky in the best places, it's five times as strong as steel and still flexible.

What do you think? Could you learn to love spiders?

Slippery evidence

A slimy trail at Düsseldorf Airport in Germany helped **customs officials** to solve an unusual crime.

Officers found a giant African land snail on the floor, and its gooey trail led directly back to some bags containing 92 other snails that were being **smuggled** to Germany from Nigeria. The silvery slime trail gave the criminals away.

DID YOU KNOW?
The word part "cent" may mean 100, but centipedes are born with between 15 and 177 pairs of legs, depending on the species.

FACT FOCUS: Stomach-foot

Slugs and snails are a kind of creature called "gastropods". "Gastro" means "stomach" and "pod" means "foot" and this sums them up well. A slug or snail's foot pulls their soft body forward, leaving a slimy trail, so that they can munch their way through plants.

EARTH'S ENVIRONMENT

EPIC AMAZON
The Amazon rainforest contains an estimated 400 billion trees and spans eight countries.

GOOD NEWS STORIES

We live in a difficult and **critical** time for the environment. However, despite the challenges to our planet, there are also good news stories for nature lovers.

Lost tree rediscovered

A type of holly tree that had been thought lost for 186 years has been rediscovered in Igarassu, Brazil.

Experts were working on a project called the "Search for Lost Species". After six days of searching, they finally spotted four Pernambuco holly trees, which they recognised from their tiny white flowers.

Sculptures built to restore coral reefs

Counting Coral, an organisation dedicated to restoring coral, has planted steel structures underwater in order to grow new coral.

Coral reefs are home to lots of ocean wildlife, but climate change has harmed much of it. Coral has been planted on the sculptures and, as it grows, parts will be snipped off and planted on reefs elsewhere.

Greta Thunberg sparks change

Research suggests that the climate protests started by Greta Thunberg in 2018 made people in Switzerland more environmentally friendly.

More than 1,200 Swiss people were asked about their habits before and after the protests, and 30% had changed them. These changes included what they bought, their recycling habits and how they travel.

Protection for sponsored sea

Niue, a tiny Pacific island nation, has announced a creative plan to protect its environment.

The island's leader, Dalton Tagelagi, is asking people and companies to sponsor sections of the ocean around Niue, in order to protect it from threats such as illegal fishing and plastic waste.

This means that they pay £120 for a square kilometre of ocean and the money goes to a charity to help protect it for 20 years. There are 127,000 square kilometre units of ocean available to sponsor. Niue will buy 1,700 of them to represent each of the island's citizens. It hopes to raise more than £14.7 million from the rest.

Tagelagi said that the people of Niue have a very close relationship with the sea.

"We live off the ocean," he said. "That's our **livelihood**."

Legal rights for nature

In 2023, sea turtles in Panama were given the legal right to live and move freely in a healthy environment.

This was a win for the "Rights of Nature" **movement**. People who back this want to give animals and other natural **entities**, like rivers or trees, the legal right to exist and thrive. It gives them the same status as humans.

The Law Society, a group that represents lawyers in England and Wales, recently wrote a report saying that Rights of Nature laws are essential for the future protection of wildlife and nature on Earth.

A RIGHT TO FLOW
New Zealand's Whanganui River is a "legal person" – so it has the same rights as a human.

The plan to boost insects

Insects are an important part of food production; they keep the soil healthy and help plants to reproduce by pollinating them.

However, insect populations across the world are falling at a rate of about 1% a year. Farming methods that use chemicals to kill certain bugs have harmed insect populations more widely.

To battle this problem, farmers in the UK are now being rewarded for using environmentally friendly farming methods. These include planting hedgerows, growing wildflowers to attract insects and introducing (or reintroducing) particular insects to eat crop-damaging bugs.

Earless dragon spotted after 50 years

In Victoria, Australia, a species of lizard believed to be extinct in the wild for 50 years has been rediscovered. Until now, experts thought that there weren't any Victorian grassland earless dragons left, except those in zoos.

The exact place they were found has been kept secret to protect them. The lizards are very small and don't have an ear opening on their heads.

Vote protects national park

In 2023, people in Ecuador voted to halt drilling for oil in Yasuní National Park, a protected area of the Amazon rainforest. The park is home to wildlife and different groups of **indigenous people**. If the government respect the results, the oil company will have to move out.

HUMANS HARMING THE WORLD

The environment needs lots of care and we all need to do what we can to stop damaging it, reduce human waste and preserve animal habitats.

Beaches are being washed away

Rising sea levels and winter storms are washing away beaches in Barcelona, Spain. The beaches aren't natural – they were created more than 30 years ago to attract tourists. Now more than 70% of the sand has gone.

Authorities have been adding extra sand each year, but some people say that this is a waste of money and bad for the environment.

FACT FOCUS: What is climate change?

Climate change is a change in the average conditions – such as temperature and rainfall – in a specific place over a long period of time. Climate change on Earth is being sped up by human activity such as burning **fossil fuels**.

In most areas, this has meant rising temperatures. They have resulted in a lot of ice melting and therefore sea levels rising. Climate change is also linked to extreme weather such as floods, **droughts** and hurricanes.

Barceloneta Beach, Barcelona, Spain.

Heavy rainfall causes major floods

In summer 2023, Nova Scotia, Canada, was hit by severe flooding, caused by the heaviest rainfall in 50 years.

Some places had more than 25 centimetres of rain in 24 hours – the same amount that usually falls in three months. The floods caused damage to roads, bridges and buildings, and more than 80,000 people were left without electricity.

Flooding in Nova Scotia, Canada.

Ice is at record low

Images taken by satellites show that Antarctic ice levels are at their lowest since records began.

Between June and September, the ocean around the continent usually has about 19 million square kilometres of floating ice. In 2023, about 1.5 million square kilometres of this was missing, which is an area seven times the size of Britain.

Ice on the Antarctic Ross Sea.

Scientists track giant icebergs

Scientists are tracking two of the world's largest icebergs, which have broken off from Antarctica. The iceberg A-76a measures just over 3,000 square kilometres, about the size of the UK county of Cornwall. A-81 is half that size.

Wind and ocean currents are driving the icebergs north, where they may cause real dangers for both ships and wildlife.

Iceberg A-76a.

Hunting in different ways

The effects of climate change are forcing some animals to adapt their hunting methods – or starve. Polar bears have reacted to melting sea ice in Greenland by hunting on blocks of freshwater ice from glaciers instead.

Increasingly hot weather has caused African wild dogs to change the time of day that they hunt in order to keep cool.

Adélie penguins in the Antarctic now travel further to find krill, their favourite food. Antarctic krill rely on ice for food and shelter so melting ice sheets have caused krill populations to shrink. This costs the penguins extra energy and means they take longer to return to their chicks.

An African wild dog.

Floating village stranded

A village that floats on water has been left stranded, after Lake Puraquequara, in the Amazon rainforest, dried up following a severe drought.

The cleverly designed buildings would usually sit above the water level and people would use boats to get to them, but everything is now stuck in the mud at the bottom of the lake.

BEATING THE HEAT

Places all over the world are heating up. Environmentalists hope that this can be stopped or at least slowed. Until then, people have to find a way to live with the heat.

Free sun cream for all

In the Netherlands, the number of people with **skin cancer**, which can be caused by the Sun's rays, has been rising.

In 2023 the Dutch government offered the public free sun cream over summer. It was available in public places, including schools, parks and sports venues.

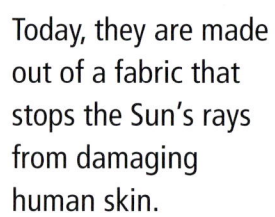

A hot new fashion

Some people are sporting a new fashion item as temperatures soar above 35°C in Beijing, China. The facekini – a mask covering the wearer's head, face and neck – was invented in 2004 by accountant Zhang Shifanan to protect swimmers from jellyfish stings.

Today, they are made out of a fabric that stops the Sun's rays from damaging human skin.

City helps the homeless

In Barcelona, Spain, the council gave homeless people hats and drinking water to help them during a particularly intense heatwave.

In 2023, temperatures in the city reached 38.8°C, breaking the 2010 record of 37.4°C. More than 3,000 people who were most at risk received text messages with advice and directions to air-conditioned areas with drinking fountains.

Oyster-shell roofs

Oysters (a type of shellfish) are a popular food in France and around the world. In fact, more than 130,000 tonnes of shells are thrown away each year.

Now, a company called Cool Roof France (CRF) has found a clever use for them. The company takes the calcium – a mineral in the shells – and adds it to special white paint. Painting it onto roofs helps to keep buildings cool in the summer.

The company says that the ground-up shells make the paint last longer and can cool the building by around 7°C.

RESTORING BALANCE

Humans have harmed the natural world by hunting animals or destroying their habitats. However, some people are working hard to reintroduce species to their original habitats – or new ones that suit them.

Most Bali myna birds are kept in zoos.

Bali myna birds take survival tests

A group of **conservationists** set bird exams to see whether Bali myna birds in UK zoos would survive well if released into the wild. The species is from Bali, an island in Indonesia, but there are fewer than 50 left in the wild.

Tests included putting jelly in the birds' enclosures to see how they reacted to unknown foods. They also faced problem-solving tests, in which they had to lift a lid or pull a string to get food.

The study found that the two Bali myna personalities most suitable for release were the boldest, which were better at solving problems, and the most cautious, which are probably better at avoiding predators.

Seahorse numbers boosted

Hundreds of White's seahorses were released into Sydney Harbour to replenish their falling population on Australia's east coast. After being fitted with tags so they could be monitored, they were released into "seahorse hotels" designed to give them the best chance of survival.

Return of the hazel dormice

Golden-coated hazel dormice used to be common in the UK's woodlands. Unfortunately, between 2000 and 2023, their numbers declined by 51%. They had become extinct in 17 English counties.

However, in 2023, wildlife charities introduced 38 captive-bred hazel dormice into woodland in Derbyshire, UK. Volunteers monitored and fed the dormice, who stayed in nest boxes in cages. If all was well after 10 days, they were free to wander.

MAKING SOMETHING FROM NOTHING

These experts and organisations are tackling the problem of waste in their own ways, by making new products from rubbish.

Sorting fashion's waste

Around the world, a lorry's worth of clothes ends up in **landfill** every second.

A second-hand clothing company called Ecocitex, based in Chile, is fighting back against fabric waste.

Ecocitex sells clothes that are still in good condition. Clothing in poor condition is made into other products, such as bags, pencil cases or thread to be used for knitting and sewing. Anything left over is used as stuffing for cushions and pillows.

From junk to jewellery

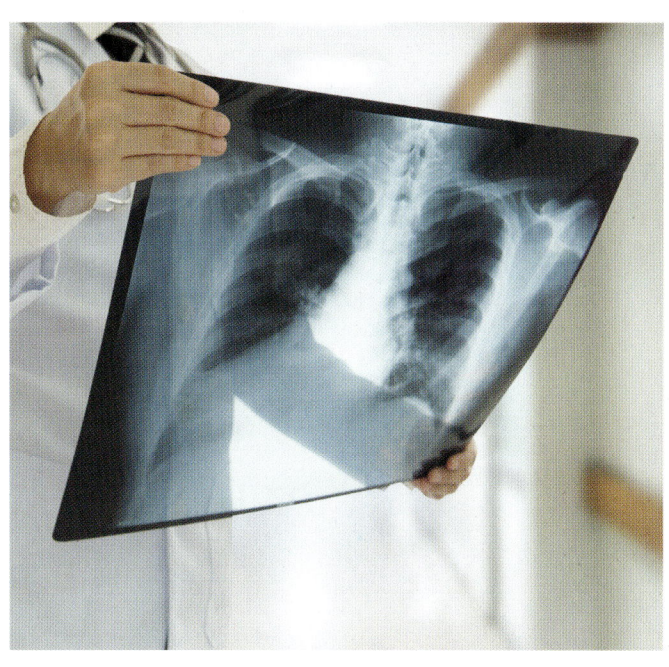

The Royal Mint, the organisation that produces UK coins and banknotes, has found a use for old **x-ray** film. The film contains small amounts of silver, which can be taken out to make jewellery.

Sean Millard from the Royal Mint said, "This means responsibly sourcing materials that have the potential to reuse our planet's precious resources."

Making toys from rubbish

A boy living in a camp for **displaced** people in Syria makes toys out of scrap materials.

Ibrahim Al-Naes and his brother Ali collect things like cans and bottles and use scissors and tools to make them into toy vehicles. Ibrahim wants to be an engineer.

Bags and bottles become soap

Scientists have discovered that the plastic bags and bottles we use in everyday life can be recycled to make soap and detergent.

The researchers found that the chemical chains that make up some plastics are a little like wax. They can be adapted into a fatty substance that makes soap.

Some soaps are made from animal fats, so using plastic to make them instead could also reduce harm to animals.

GOING GREEN

Helping to fight pollution can be as easy as riding a bike.

Two wheels (or legs), not four

Every September, World Car Free Day encourages people to leave their cars at home and explore where they live by walking or cycling. Joining in could be as simple as taking a bus instead of being driven, as shared transport reduces car traffic.

If you'd like to celebrate the special day by heading out further on two wheels, you could ask an adult to look up Sustrans, which is the organisation that is in charge of the UK's National Cycle Network.

The network includes more than 12,000 miles of routes for cycling. Its website helps you to find cycling routes wherever you are in the UK.

FACT FOCUS: Reducing traffic

Road traffic creates harmful **emissions**. Many vehicles rely on precious fossil fuels, which are mined from the ground, damaging it. Everyone can help to reduce traffic on our roads.

A battery-free ebike

The first battery-free electric bike (ebike) was designed by a company in Orléans, France.

The bike has a **supercapacitor**, a device that stores electric power differently from the way a battery does. It recharges when riders pedal on flat surfaces, go down hills or brake.

A supercapacitor is much greener than the batteries in most ebikes. Those are usually made with lithium, a material that is taken from the ground – a process that can damage the environment.

Re-Cycle

By sending bikes to Africa, Re-Cycle changes lives. For many people in Africa, bicycles are the only form of transport (due to a lack of cars or public transport outside cities).

Rather than choosing to build new bike factories, Re-Cycle reuses old bikes, either by repairing and refreshing them or by using their parts. They can be a lifeline for people who can't afford to pay for transport. They have other benefits too – including fewer factories and less landfill. You could donate unwanted bikes to Re-Cycle or choose to fundraise for the **scheme**.

Saving power at home

Saving power at home has two benefits. As well as saving your family money, it reduces the need for fuels used to make electricity.

Turn off lights

When you leave a room, turn off the lights. In the evening, try to wait as long as you can to turn them on. You could also challenge your family to use **LED bulbs** instead of **filament bulbs**, as these use less power.

Layer up and jump around

Before turning the heating on or up, try other ways to keep warm, such as putting on a jumper or a pair of fluffy socks.

If you sit still for a while, you may start to feel cold. To warm up, try doing star jumps. Your body will quickly generate heat. How many star jumps does it take for you to get warm?

Find the blasts

Cold blasts of air that breeze through gaps in doors and windows can make rooms chilly.

Track down where the cold air is entering using a "tissue test". Hold a piece of tissue by any doors and windows where cool air might be coming in. If the tissue is fluttering, you've discovered a draught.

Measure up

Hot drinks are a great way to warm up in winter. However, a full kettle can waste electricity and money. It costs around seven times more to boil a full kettle, than to boil a kettle with one mug of water in it.

By measuring the exact amount of water you need and pouring it into the kettle, you could save money and energy.

Eco-friendly tips

These five simple habits can help you to protect Earth all year long.

Avoid plastics

Disposable plastic items, like bags, water bottles and straws, end up in landfills after one use and take years to break down. Instead, carry reusable versions with you.

Save paper

Instead of drawing or writing notes on a new pad of paper, use the back of something you've already written on, or an envelope or flyer that came in the post.

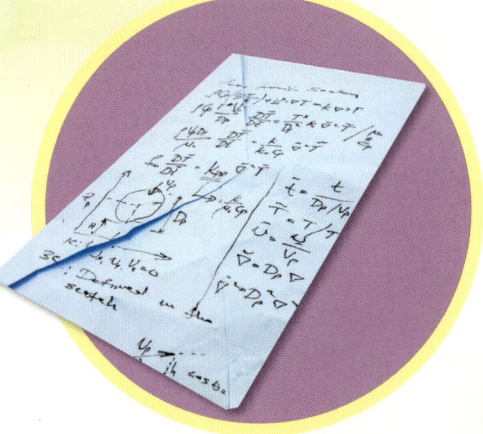

Conserve water

Taking short showers and turning off the tap while you're brushing your teeth can save litres of water a day.

Attend an event

Earth Day is celebrated every year on 22nd April. Celebration days like this help environmental causes by raising awareness and often raising money for related charities.

On and around Earth Day, people across the world gather at special events.

Common options include participating in a march or rally to raise awareness of climate change, attending an arts workshop, or taking a nature walk.

You can find events in your area by asking an adult to look up the Earth Day website.

Get planting

One way your family can invest in the planet is by planting a tree. Growing trees helps to clean the air by absorbing **carbon dioxide** and releasing oxygen.

You can check with your local council to find out if they already have a tree-planting programme (you may be able to get a tree for free).

You can also plant flowers and vegetables in a garden. Growing vegetables also creates another way to reduce pollution: you can eat the food you grow and reduce the need for food to be transported to and from shops.

Waste not, want not

It can make a big difference to keep the "five Rs" in mind: refuse, reduce, reuse, repurpose and recycle. Here are a few R-based activities you could enjoy.

Craft beads from waste paper

Curl a paper strip around a cocktail stick, adding little blobs of glue to hold the paper in place as you wrap it. Repeat to create lots of beads, and thread them onto elastic to make a necklace or bracelet.

To create beads with rounded sides, cut your strips into long, thin triangles rather than oblongs. Start wrapping from the wide end.

Turn a tin into a bird feeder

Ask an adult to make a hole in the bottom of an empty tin to the side. Thread a stick through the hole, making sure that it's long enough to poke out the open side by around 10 centimetres. Tie string around the tin, add some seed and hang it outside. You could decorate the tin however you like.

Make vegetable-peel crisps

Cover peelings from well-scrubbed **root vegetables** with oil, salt and any spices you like (such as cumin or paprika).

Ask an adult to help you spread them on a baking tray, and bake them for 15 to 20 minutes at 190°C. Turn them halfway through, and make sure that they don't burn.

Host a clothing swap

Plan a day with friends to swap clothes that you no longer wear. If each person brings a bundle of clean clothes, you can swap items to make sure that yours get a new home – and you could come away with some new looks.

There are other things you can do with old clothes, such as using them for cleaning, to wrap gifts and to make a **quilt**.

Use the fabric to wrap gifts.

Cut up old clothes for cleaning rags.

Use squares of different fabric to make a quilt.

PEOPLE POWER

SPEEDY DESCENT
Professional speed skydivers can reach speeds of up to 329 miles per hour.

DAREDEVILS

Humans can impress in hundreds of thousands of ways. Some of the most attention-grabbing actions are daredevil stunts like these.

Pilot leaps from plane to plane

A daredevil pilot jumped from one plane to another in mid-air.

Luke Aikins wanted to become the first person to perform the stunt. Aikins, who is also an experienced skydiver, took on the challenge with his cousin Andy Farrington. The pair flew side by side and planned to jump to each other's planes.

Aikins succeeded, but Farrington felt that he couldn't make it. He opened his parachute instead, and floated back down to earth.

Aikins said of the stunt, "There's no way to test it until you do it."

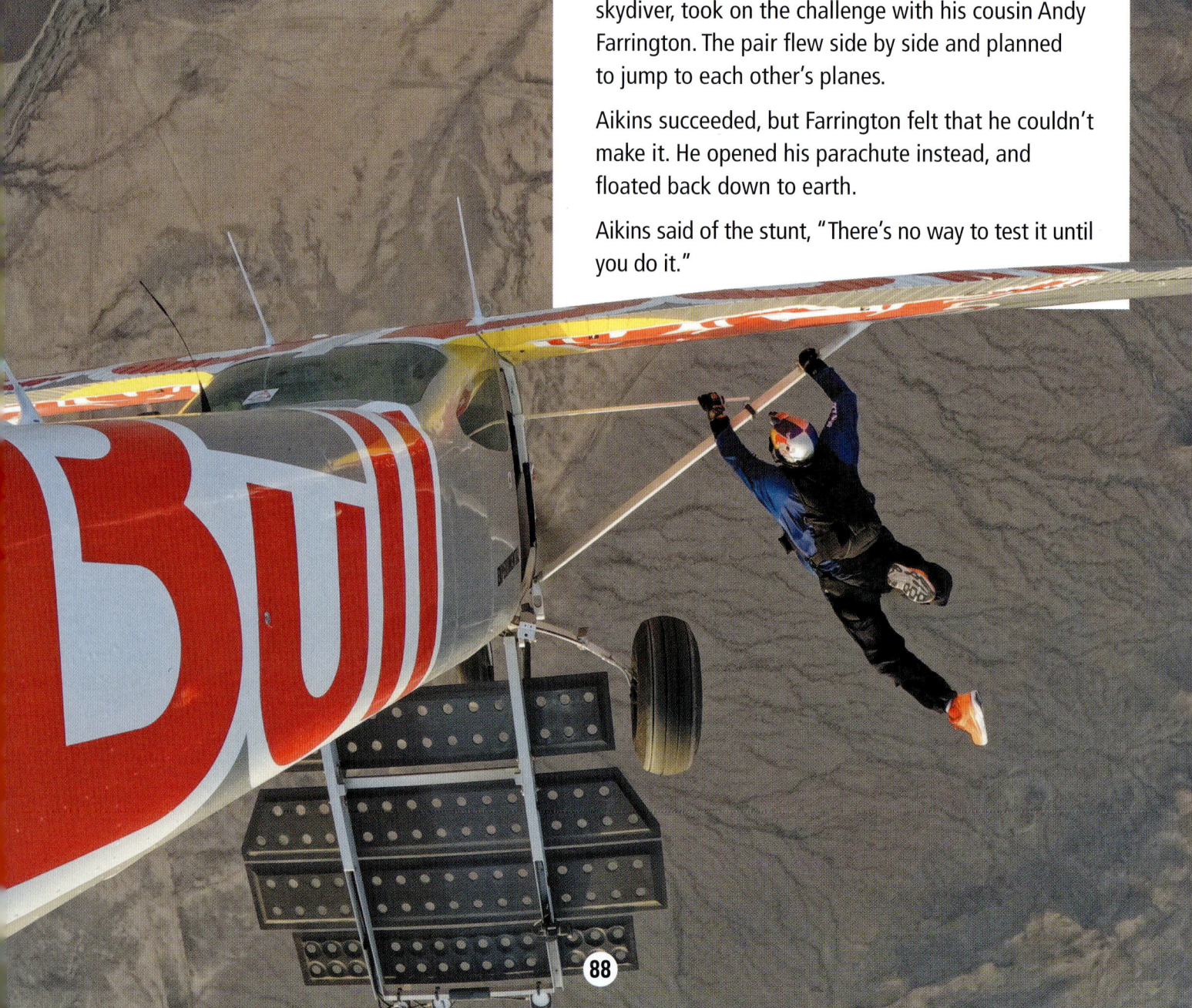

Pianist puts on a daring performance

As an adventurous pianist, Alain Roche, is known for taking his music to new heights. In fact, he recently performed a concert while hovering in the air above a building site in France.

Roche and his piano were held by cables, and he played while looking up towards the sky. The musician said that he wanted to work with "mechanical, metallic" sounds and that the dirt and grit on the building site contrasted well with the shiny, polished piano. Roche gave his first "vertical" concert over 10 years ago, and has toured far and wide with his unusual act.

The 91-year-old daredevil

For a 91st birthday treat, Margaret Carroll's family gave her a ride on the world's fastest **zip wire**, whizzing over Penrhyn Quarry in Wales at nearly 100 miles per hour.

Carroll was no stranger to adventure though. During her life, she'd swum with stingrays, ridden a horse in the Grand Canyon and climbed Yr Wyddfa (Snowdon) in Wales.

Penrhyn Quarry, Wales.

Acrobatics among the clouds

Rafael Bridi is walking on air. He broke records by walking along a fabric tightrope strip between two hot air balloons, 1,900 metres above the ground. The balloons were about 18 metres apart and the adventurer walked barefoot.

"Maximum **inspiration** comes from the most unimaginable dreams," Bridi wrote on social media.

Bridi also performed a sensational stunt alongside fellow skywalker Erika Sedlacek.

The daring duo teetered along a 2.5-centimetre-wide, 510-metre-long tightrope, 114 metres above the city streets of São Paulo in Brazil.

Human snowflakes in the sky

The sky is no limit for a group of 101 California skydivers, all of whom are at least 60 years old.

In 2023, they created the largest snowflake formation while in free fall. The next day, they aimed for another record when 95 senior skydivers changed their formation mid-fall.

Patricia Brown, a 72-year-old group member, said, "You're never too old to do something that you want to do."

The skydiver and the unicorn

"I'm coming for ya!" shouted skydiver Jan Zackl as he parachuted towards an inflatable unicorn. He landed perfectly on the unicorn's back, and together they slid across a field on a slippery runway.

Zackl performed the feat at a skydiving festival in the UK. All the thrill seekers who took part were experienced skydivers who had performed at least 200 jumps, but only Zackl managed to land on the unicorn successfully.

It required great skill in canopy piloting: the sport of flying very small parachutes that move quickly. Landing is "the fun part" of a dive, Zackl said.

Daredevil walks the wire again

In 1974, Philippe Petit made headlines around the globe when he walked a tightrope between the two towers of the World Trade Centre in New York City, US.

At age 73, Petit was still amazing audiences. The fearless high-wire artist walked a 30-metre-long tightrope across the great hall of the National Building Museum in Washington DC, US. He paused in the middle only to toss glitter into the air.

His body may have aged, but Petit said, "My mind is becoming younger every day, and my passion is not fading."

REMARKABLE RESCUES

People are great at getting themselves into dangerous situations ... luckily there are also people who will go to great lengths to help others.

Location: **Morca, Turkey**
Rescued from: **Cave**

A US explorer was rescued from a cave after he fell ill and was unable to make his way out. Mark Dickey became unwell on 2 September, when he was almost 1,040 metres underground.

Dickey was no stranger to deep caving, having enjoyed many similar explorations for more than 20 years beforehand. However, when illness struck him, he feared he would never get out.

About 200 people helped in the rescue operation, which took more than a week. When he **emerged**, Dickey said that it felt "amazing" to be above ground.

Morca Cave, Turkey.

Location: **Antarctica**

Rescued from: **Remote research centre**

An urgent rescue operation collected a member of an Antarctic research team who fell ill while working in a **remote** area.

Dangerous weather prevented aeroplanes and helicopters from flying all the way from Australia to the research station in Antarctica. Instead, an **icebreaker** sailed nearly 3,000 kilometres from Australia to reach it.

The ship brought a helicopter that then carried the man the short distance to the ship. There, a medical team helped him before he was transferred to a hospital in Australia.

The icebreaker RSV Nuyina.

Location: **Colombia**

Rescued from: **Amazon rainforest**

After a 40-day search, rescuers found four children who were lost in the Amazon rainforest.

The three sisters, aged 13, nine and one, and their five-year-old brother were in a plane that crashed in the middle of the jungle. Three adults who were also on the plane, including their mother, did not survive the accident.

The children were travelling to Bogotá, Colombia's capital, to join their father. The children are Huitoto people, a group who live in the remote Amazonas region of Colombia. They knew some survival skills, including what was safe to eat in the jungle.

They hid in tree trunks to avoid dangerous animals and survived on berries, seeds and a bag of flour left on the plane.

A team of 100 soldiers and 70 volunteers, including their father, searched for the children. They followed clues like scissors, a nappy and a bottle. They worked night and day in difficult conditions.

Finally, they sent out a message over the radio: "Miracle, miracle, miracle, miracle." "Miracle" was the code word for each child found alive.

The army officer in charge of the search was later asked to become the godfather of the one-year-old baby. Colombia's president, Gustavo Petro, said that the story "would be remembered in history".

Location: **Battagram, Pakistan**

Rescued from: **Cable car**

In August 2023, six children and two adults were rescued after being stranded for 14 hours in a cable car that was used by local people to get to schools and shops. After one of its cables snapped, the passengers were trapped 275 metres above the ground.

Strong winds made it difficult for helicopters to approach, but the army's rescue team managed to get food and medicine to the trapped passengers. Eventually, one passenger was rescued by helicopter and the others via a zip line.

FANTASTIC FINDS

Humans are fascinated by **prehistory**. These amazing accidental finds suggest just how much there is to discover.

Old bones lead to new discovery

Ancient human bones found in a cave in Laos are evidence that humans lived in Asia much earlier than historians thought.

Researchers stumbled on what they thought was a big stone. To clear the way, they moved it. They saw that it was white underneath, and realised it was part of a human skull. They also found a shin bone.

Previously, it was thought that humans first journeyed out of Africa around 50,000 years ago, moving into Asia and other places.

These bones show that people could have been living in Asia more than 80,000 years ago.

Dinosaur footprints once hidden under water are revealed.

Mega megalodon finds

On a seaside fossil-hunting trip to Essex, UK, 13-year-old Ben Evans and his dad found a giant tooth.

Ben wants to be a **palaeontologist**, so knows something about ancient creatures. His dad said, "Ben knew straight away that it was something."

Experts confirmed what Ben thought. The tooth was from a type of giant prehistoric shark called a megalodon.

Meanwhile, nine-year-old Molly Sampson from Maryland, US, put her passions – and presents – to good use.

She received fossil-hunting tools on Christmas morning. Later that day, at the coast, she found a five-inch tooth from a megalodon.

Molly sent the tooth to a museum, which called it "a spectacular **specimen**".

Dinosaur footprints revealed

In 2023, 110-million-year-old dinosaur tracks were found in the state of Texas, US.

They belonged to two types of dinosaurs: the *Acrocanthosaurus*, which looked a bit like a *Tyrannosaurus rex*, and the long-necked *Sauroposeidon*.

This evidence that these dinosaurs existed in the area was seen only due to the weather. The footprints had been hidden under water and mud, which hot and dry weather had dried up.

Human history

Ancient human records teach us even more about who we are.

The ancient city of Pompeii.

The people of Pompeii

In the year 79 **CE**, the Italian city of Pompeii was buried under hot ash when a nearby volcano, Mount Vesuvius, erupted.

What **archaeologists** have uncovered is astonishing. The ash preserved the city in great detail, from the houses to food.

Archaeologists have found an ancient bread oven, leftovers from a meal and the burnt remains of a bed. Wall paintings and **mosaics** were uncovered, including one showing Latin words meaning "beware of the dog".

The Sutton Hoo treasure

One of the famous collections in the British Museum, the Sutton Hoo treasure, was found in a 27-metre-long ship beneath an Anglo-Saxon burial mound in Suffolk, UK.

On display is gold jewellery, silverware, ornate dinner sets and a unique helmet, thought to have belonged to an important man, perhaps a king.

Roman swords found

Researchers discovered four Roman swords in a cave near the Dead Sea, a large salty desert lake. The cave is very cool and dry, preserving the swords well.

As one expert, Guy Stiebel, said, each sword "can tell you an entire story". Experts think that the swords were seized from the Roman army by **rebels** who followed the Jewish faith, during a war around 1,900 years ago.

The Young Archaeologists' Club

Would you like to spend some spare time digging around in the dirt, looking for treasures from the past? The Young Archaeologists' Club can help. It's a network of clubs around the UK that help young people to get involved in digs.

To find out more, ask an adult to look up their website.

ANGLO-SAXONS RULE! Anglo-Saxons ruled much of England from the sixth century BCE until 1066.

SENSATIONAL SCIENCE

HOME PLANETS?
Experts think that our Milky Way galaxy could contain 40 billion planets similar to Earth.

INCREDIBLE AI

What is AI?

AI is a computer system that can do things that usually require human intelligence. These include solving problems, making decisions and learning.

AI can be taught skills using a process called "machine learning". Humans give the system information, such as books, photos or videos, to train it. The more data the system studies, the better it can do its job.

AI and robotics aren't the same – not all robots are intelligent. Some are just programmed to carry out basic tasks that don't require intelligence.

Intelligence, reason and logic

Perhaps it is no surprise that AI excels at some things. It's able to analyse lots of information at once, and compare it to see patterns.

AI is very good at suggesting drugs to treat diseases, and can even invent new medicines. It can also fight climate change by finding clever ways to reduce our energy use and helping us to get more out of solar panels and wind turbines.

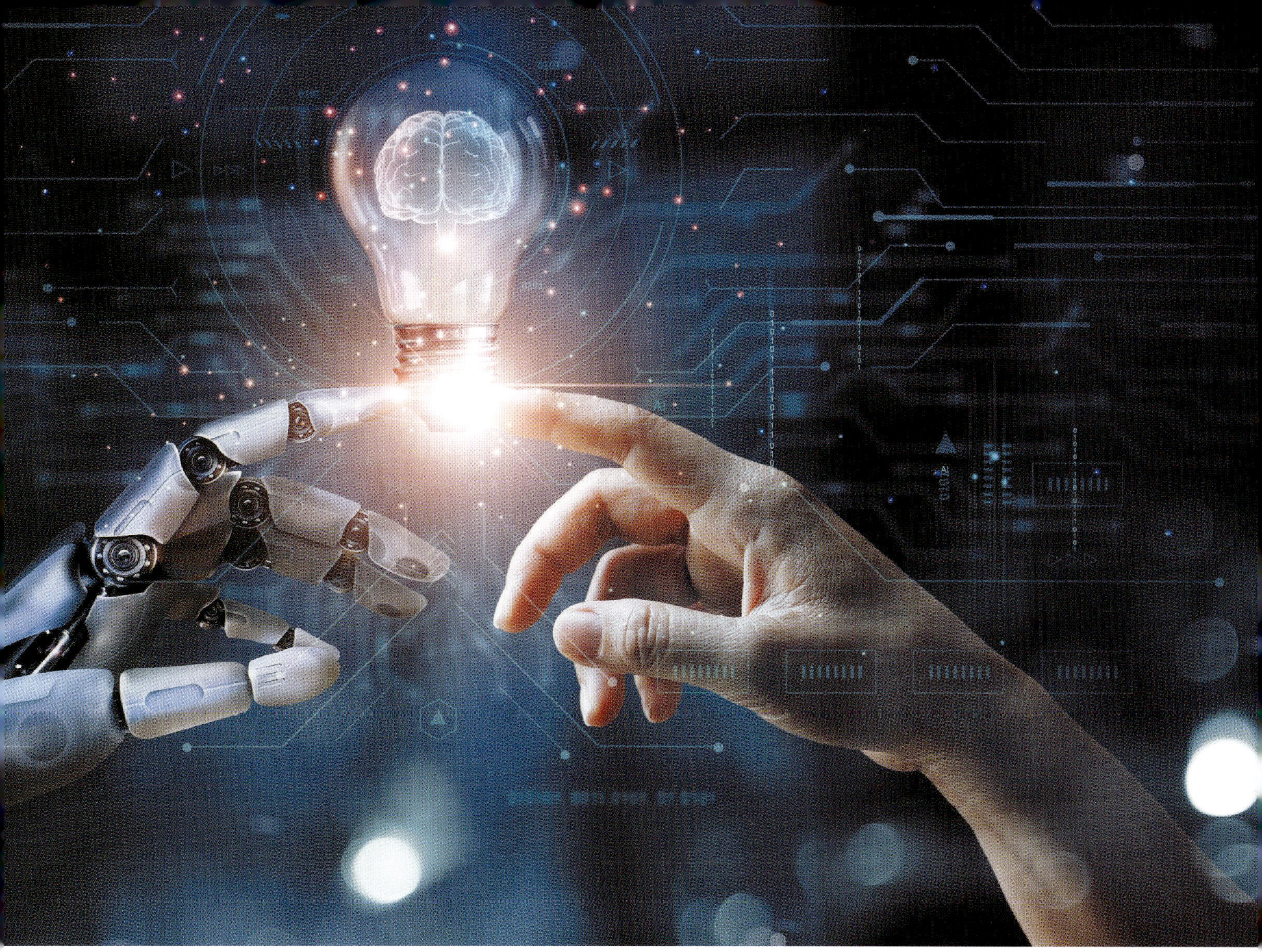

Atlas the agile robot

Boston Dynamics in Massachusetts, US, have used AI technology to create a **humanoid** with very lifelike movements. The 1.5-metre-tall robot, called Atlas, was able to use its legs to walk, run and even jump.

In 2024, Boston Dynamics announced that they had retired this version of Atlas in favour of a fully electric version. The new Atlas will be stronger and will have a greater range of motion.

Artificially artistic?

Despite AI's benefits, some people worry about how it might affect their jobs. If computers can create images, music and text, could artists, musicians and writers one day be replaced?

Bringing a band back to life

More than 50 years ago, a famous British band called the Beatles split up. They haven't recorded any music together since then. However, in 2023, band member Paul McCartney used AI to create one last song "with" his co-founder John Lennon, who died in 1980. McCartney developed an old unfinished song created by the Beatles with the help of AI that had learned the Beatles' style and had access to all the sounds from their other music.

AI discovers a hidden masterpiece

The National Library in Madrid, Spain, uses AI to copy out the old books and writings in its collection.

The AI bot worked out that one of the texts that it was copying was a previously unknown play by one of the country's greatest writers, Lope de Vega, by recognising the writer's style but not the text's content.

Robots show off their skills

Every year, tech companies gather in Beijing, China, for the annual World Robot Conference to view the latest developments in robotics and how they could be used in everyday life.

At a recent conference, some robots were able to draw portraits of visitors, while others served ice cream, gave people back massages or scanned people for illnesses.

SWITCHED ON OR SILENT?

Our smart devices keep us in touch, informed and entertained. Not everyone welcomes them everywhere though – and device bans are becoming more common.

A distraction-free zone

Pupils in the Netherlands are no longer able to use devices such as smartphones, tablets and smart watches in the classroom. The ban, which came into force in January 2024, is aimed at stopping pupils from being distracted.

The Dutch education minister, Robbert Dijkgraaf, said, "Students need to be able to concentrate."

No smarts at school

The parents of pupils at eight primary schools in Greystones, Ireland, have decided to ban smartphones at home as well as school.

Under this voluntary scheme, children won't be allowed to have smartphones until they go to secondary school. The aim is to reduce the anxiety and stress caused by being online too much.

The parents and schools hope that if none of the children have phones, no one will feel left out.

Phone-free zone

A small Finnish island called Ulko-Tammio has declared itself a phone-free zone. Tourists are encouraged to switch off their phones so they can connect with nature.

How to take a break from tech:

1. Set boundaries. If you reach for your device every time you're bored, that might be a sign to take time away. Set yourself limits for how long to use it each day or in one go.

2. Delete **addictive** apps. Get rid of apps that keep grabbing your attention and hold your focus for too long – even if it's just temporarily. You could also stop notifications.

3. Give yourself mini breaks. If you're on a device to do homework, avoid being distracted by taking planned breaks: do 20 minutes of homework and then allow yourself five minutes to check messages. (Then take another five to get up and stretch!)

MAKING ENDS MEAT

The ethics of eating meat is a hot topic. What if meat didn't have to come from animals, though? Advances in technology mean that meat grown in labs is now a reality.

Safari burgers for supper

Lion meat grown in a lab could soon be sold in the UK.

A company called Primeval Foods says that instead of farming exotic animals, it grows their cells in a lab. These are used to make artificial meat that tastes the same as the real thing, but doesn't harm the environment or animals.

If the food passes its health checks, the company also hopes to offer elephant, tiger and zebra-flavoured sushi.

Yilmaz Bora of Primeval Foods said that the company hopes "to give the world a taste of what the next chapter of food would look like".

Mmm ... mammoth meatballs

Some scientists believe that the future of food lies in the distant past. The Australian company Vow has grown a meatball using DNA from woolly mammoths.

Vow hopes that lab-grown mammoth meat will be better for the environment than using meat from farm animals. Researchers have already investigated the possibility of growing meat from other DNA, including from alpacas, kangaroos and peacocks.

However, a Vow scientist revealed that even they hesitated to eat the mammoth meatball, because they had "no idea how our immune system would react".

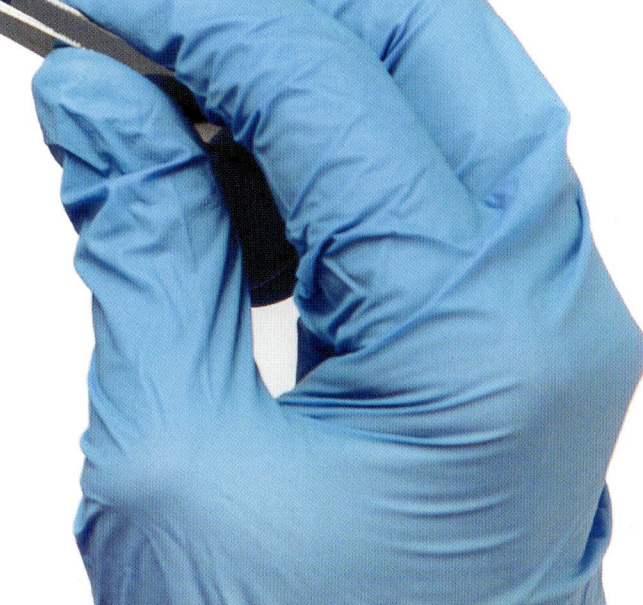

Lab-grown meat

Different governments have reacted very differently to the idea of lab-grown meat. Singapore and the US were the first countries to give companies permission to sell it.

However, Italy's government decided to ban it. They said that this was to protect traditions and farmers, and because providers couldn't guarantee the same quality as natural meat.

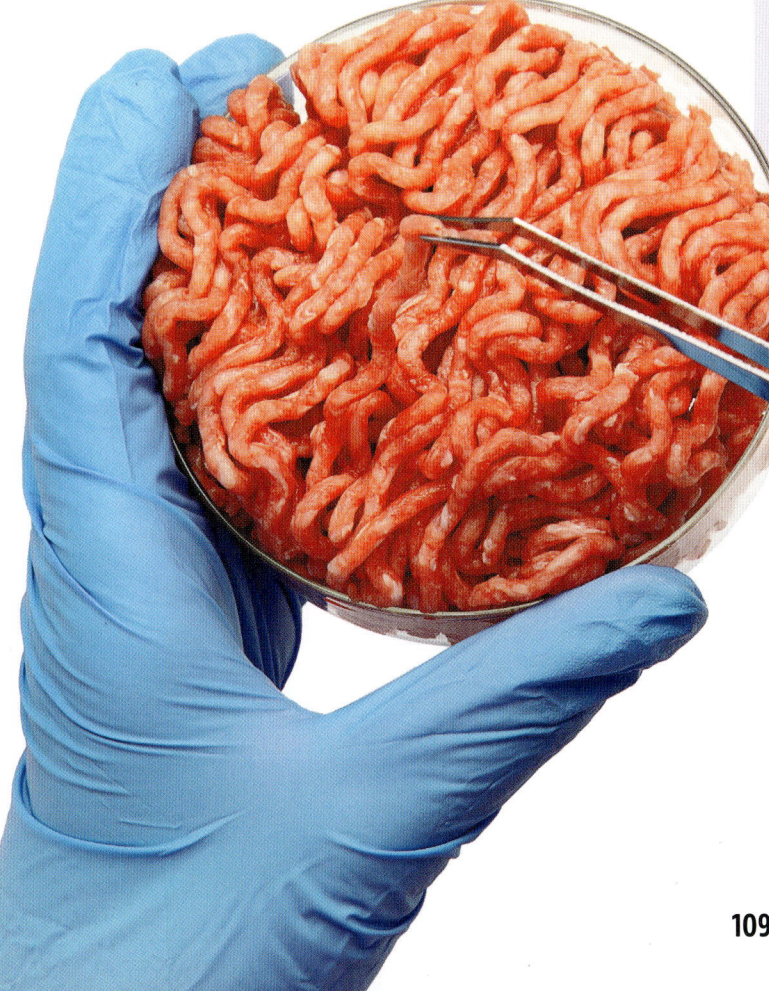

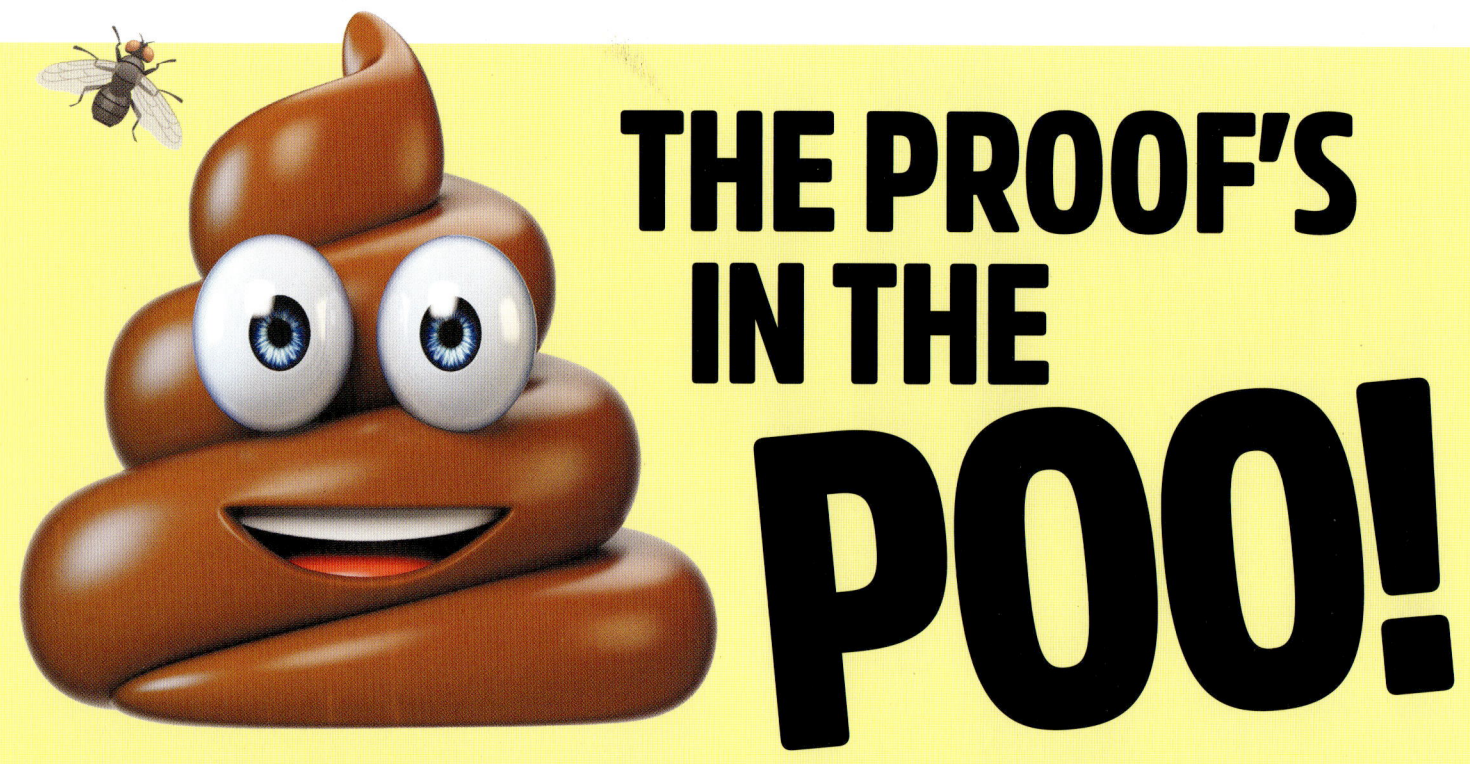

THE PROOF'S IN THE POO!

Think that all poo's just flushed and forgotten? Think again. Poo can provide powerful proof for scientists. It can even save lives.

Poos against polio

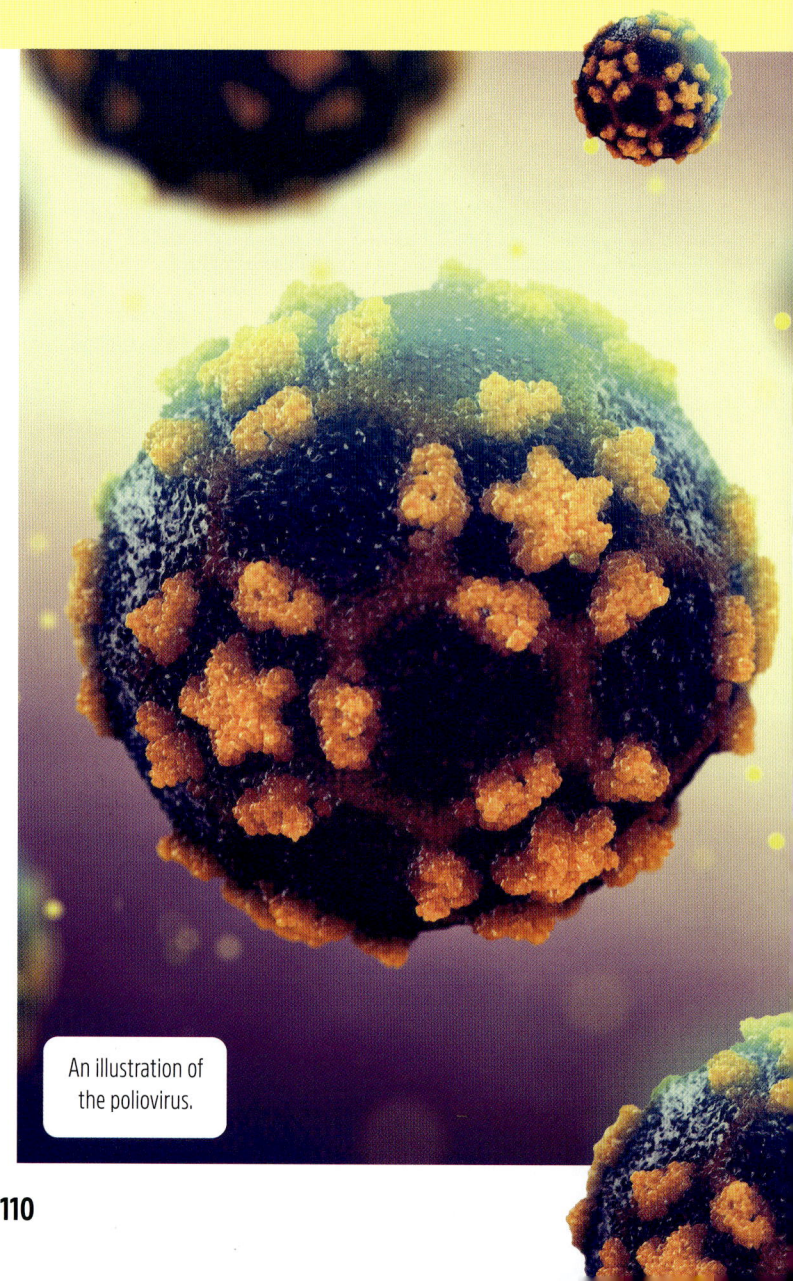

Poliovirus, the germ that causes an illness called polio, can now be detected quickly and easily, thanks to a new method: testing poo.

Some people with polio feel no effect at all. However, it can cause breathing difficulties, **paralysis** and even death.

Many countries prevent polio by giving everyone a vaccine when they're young. However, not all places do – so it's important to detect the disease.

The poo test is much quicker than other tests. Importantly, it can also check whole areas at once through their **sewage**. It's accurate in more than 99% of cases.

An illustration of the poliovirus.

Spot the dog

A scheme in Béziers, France, uses pooey proof against people who leave their dog's waste in the street.

Owners have to register their dog's DNA with **local authorities**. Any dog poo found can then be tested to see which dog did it.

Owners can be charged over £100 for not clearing up after their pet.

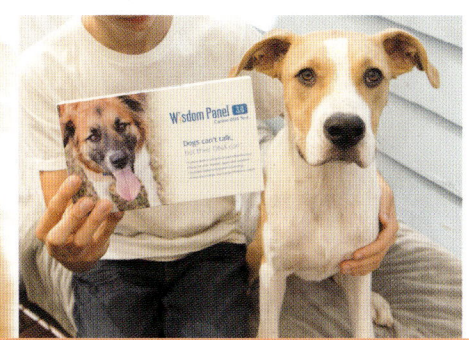

Real OR rubbish?

Dog owners offered £5,000 for sniffing poo

A company that makes plant-based dog food offered £5,000 to a dog owner for testing their dog's droppings in a particularly stinky way – through a sniff test!

The company wanted to see whether the switch from meat to plants made a difference to the smell of a pet's poo. The owner was asked to report on changes of smell, consistency and the general wellbeing of the dog.

What do you think? Is this true or does something smell bad about it?*

* **Real!** As well as £5,000 for two months of sniffing, the company offered to cover the cost of the dog food and provide an expert to monitor the dog's health.

SPACE: STRANGER THAN SCIENCE FICTION

Journeying into space is far from dull – so why sleep through it? **NASA** astronauts (and astro-rodents) may have no choice.

An undercover mission

In the 2030s, NASA aims to land humans on Mars. The journey could take around nine months. That's quite a long time – but what if the astronauts didn't have to spend those nine months awake and waiting? Instead, could they go into a hibernation-like state for the journey and wake up once they get there?

A group of scientists has been testing to see whether they might be able to send the astronauts into a state called "torpor", which is similar to hibernation.

Experts have been able to send mice into torpor using **ultrasound** waves. However, mice enter that state naturally if the weather is cold or food is short. Humans don't, so creating torpor will be more difficult.

Scientists are beginning to test the effectiveness of ultrasound waves on rats, which don't hibernate – but that will be a long mission in itself.

Vladyslav Vyazovskiy, a scientist who studies sleep, said that until human hibernation is understood, the plan should "remain in the **domain** of science fiction".

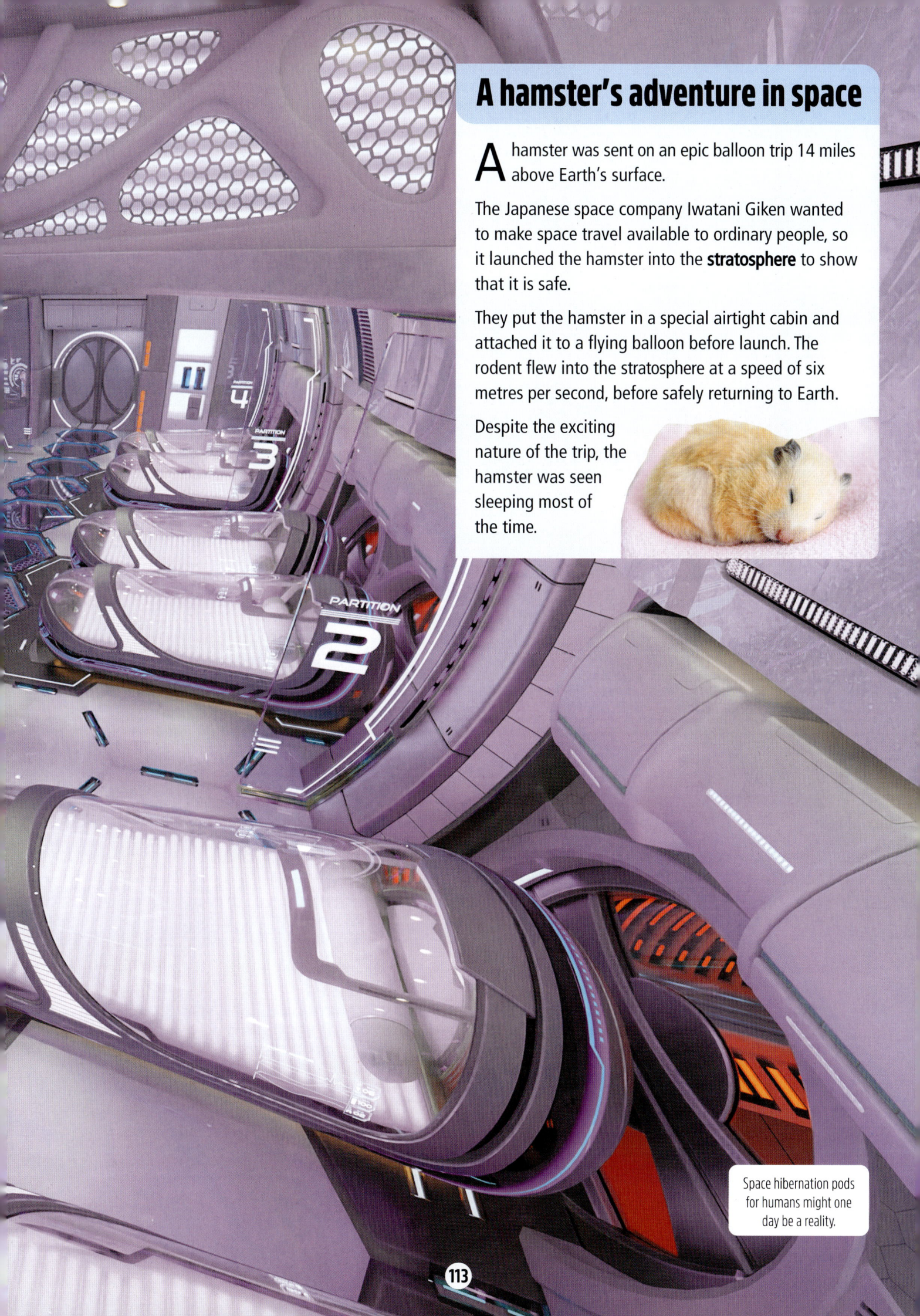

A hamster's adventure in space

A hamster was sent on an epic balloon trip 14 miles above Earth's surface.

The Japanese space company Iwatani Giken wanted to make space travel available to ordinary people, so it launched the hamster into the **stratosphere** to show that it is safe.

They put the hamster in a special airtight cabin and attached it to a flying balloon before launch. The rodent flew into the stratosphere at a speed of six metres per second, before safely returning to Earth.

Despite the exciting nature of the trip, the hamster was seen sleeping most of the time.

Space hibernation pods for humans might one day be a reality.

NASA changes asteroid path

In 2022, NASA scientists again achieved something that sounds like a science-fiction story. They changed the path of an **asteroid** by deliberately smashing a spacecraft into it.

When an asteroid hit Earth 66 million years ago, it wiped out 75% of life on the planet, including the big dinosaurs. NASA's aim was to prove that it's possible to protect Earth from any space rocks that might be heading our way.

On 26 September, the DART spacecraft crashed into a 160-metre-wide asteroid called Dimorphos, which was about 6.8 million miles from Earth.

Dimorphos was orbiting a larger space rock named Didymos, and before the crash it took 11 hours and 55 minutes to complete one circuit. For the mission to be considered a success, that orbit time had to change by at least 73 seconds.

In fact, it changed by 32 minutes – confirming that the idea could one day be used to save Earth.

Bill Nelson, who is the chief of NASA, was delighted. He explained, "NASA has proven we are serious as a defender of the planet."

ROTATING MOON
The Moon rotates once every time it orbits Earth, so we always see the same side of the Moon.

Space outlaws

In 2022, Canada passed a law meaning that Canadian astronauts committing crimes in space would be treated as if they were still in Canada.

The law meant that astronauts would be punished by Canadian law for any crimes that they committed either on the Moon or on a ship anywhere in space – so Canada's astronauts had better behave themselves.

BRILLIANT BOOKS

READING MAKES YOU HAPPY

Research by the UK charity the National Literacy Trust shows that children who read regularly tend to be happier than those who don't.

LOVE YOUR LIBRARIES

Libraries are some of the most magical places on Earth. They provide a wealth of knowledge, offer an escape into other worlds and create opportunities for everyone.

A very long-lost book

A UK library was surprised to receive the book of a lifetime – a lifetime of late fees, that is. Paddy Riordan had found a copy of Red Deer by Richard Jefferies, checked out by his grandfather in 1938.

The dutiful grandson went to the library to return the overdue book and donate £18.27 – the amount that his grandfather would have owed in late fees after 84 years.

The fee for Riordan's return seems like nothing compared to the biggest library fine recorded: it was £203.29, for a poetry book that was returned 47 years late.

Become a library expert

If you're new to using libraries, or even if you use them all the time, these tips will help you to get the most out of them.

PLENTY OF PAGES
The British Library holds around 170 million items, which fill around 463 miles of shelves.

1. Join the club

To borrow books and other items from your local library, you will need to join and get a library card. This keeps track of what books you have taken out and when they are due to be returned.

Each library will have their own rules, but usually you can borrow up to 20 books for two weeks. When your time is up, you can either return your books or renew them. Many libraries offer an online service for renewals, which is handy because there is often a charge if you don't return books on time.

2. Search for books

Entering a library to find a specific book can be **daunting**. As there are often thousands of books to sift through, librarians have created an organised system to help you to find things quickly.

Once you've found the right area for the book you want, you'll find that they're ordered alphabetically by the first three letters of the author's name, or by title if no author is given.

You can also just browse the shelves and see what you discover.

3. Use librarians' knowledge

Librarians know lots about books. If you're stuck trying to find, for example, "a yellow book about a spy written by an author that begins with P", the chances are that they'll be able to find what you're looking for.

Librarians can also make great suggestions. Tell them what you've read and enjoyed – and what you haven't – as well as the things that interest and inspire you, and they'll be able to recommend your next read.

Public libraries are priceless

The exact value of libraries is impossible to calculate, but experts have made an astonishing estimate. A report by the University of East Anglia, published in July 2023, says that the activities and services that England's libraries offer are worth £3.4 billion a year.

The team looked at how much other organisations charge for similar services, for example, and the impact that library services had on people's lives.

They included projects run by libraries – such as improving children's reading skills and helping refugees – which provide valuable benefits to society.

The researchers also found that people visit libraries to help them to feel less lonely.

Isobel Hunter, the head of Libraries Connected, hopes that the report will change how local authorities think about libraries. She said, "The evidence is clear: investing in libraries brings huge returns for local communities and the public purse."

There's a huge variety of other services that libraries also offer for free, such as:

helping people to secure jobs,

computer tutorials for older people,

yoga lessons,

classes improving adults' literacy skills.

FACT FOCUS

Covid-19

During the Covid-19 pandemic in 2020–2021, library use fell because people stayed at home. However, by the end of 2022, library use was actually higher than before.

Starfield Library in Seoul, South Korea.

READY TO READ?

Books are more than words on a page. A book can give you new skills, take you to a new place and transform you into a different person as you read.

Travel through time and space

Launch yourself into another world – maybe a fantasy land of elves and goblins or an ancient time of fierce warriors and fire-breathing dragons.

Think about what it would be like to live in that time or place. What is life like for the people and creatures who live there?

You could draw the world on a piece of paper, dress up as your favourite character or write about the experiences of people in this land.

Make the real world disappear

Listening to an audiobook can make everyday reality fade away. Your headphones are like a magic shield, protecting you from real life so that you can escape into a story as you lie in bed at home, wait at a busy airport or go on a long car journey. If you concentrate on what's going on in the book, you'll soon feel as if you are somewhere else entirely.

Learn to read minds

Use a book to put yourself in the mind of another person. It could be a magician with the power to cast spells or a spy for a top-secret organisation. Think about the character.

- What will they do when they're older?
- What would it be like to be friends with them?
- What do they enjoy doing in their spare time?

You could try writing a bit more of the story to see how their life unfolds.

TALES THAT TALK
The first audiobook was recorded in 1932 as a way for blind people to enjoy books.

Top tips for ready readers

Find your next reading adventure

When you've turned the final page of a book you love, it can be hard to know where to look next. Try these helpful hints.

- Narrow things down by choosing a **genre** you enjoy. Will it be fantasy fiction, non-fiction, mystery, horror or **realism**?

- Ask for recommendations. You could start with your friends, but try talking to librarians about what you like reading, too. They know a lot about what's on their shelves.

- Keep a list. As you're coming up with book ideas, make notes. When you have three to five books on your list, pick one to read. You can always go back to the others later.

- Take the pressure off. You won't love every book you read, and that's ok. No matter how far along you are in the book you are reading, if you don't like it, it's fine to stop reading it. You've just freed yourself up to choose another book – which could be your next favourite.

Make a cosy reading space

Find a light, quiet space away from noisy areas. In summer, you could go to the park or a back garden. Get comfy with cushions, a blanket or even a hammock. Stay refreshed with healthy drinks and snacks.

Buddy up

Finding a reading buddy builds friendships and exercises your imagination. Just like going to the beach or watching a film with someone else, reading a book together involves sharing an experience.

Reading alongside others means that you explore new worlds together. It could also help you to learn new words and ideas, and give you the confidence to explain your own feelings more easily.

READY TO WRITE?

Any writer has to start as a reader – and every reader could become a writer. If you're ready to begin your transformation, read on a little more first.

Share your story

Research shows that telling stories can improve mental health by giving the storyteller a way to share emotions and feelings rather than bottling them up.

If you write a character working through the emotions, it can help you to understand difficult feelings and, over time, it can make you moreaware of why you feel or behave a certain way.

Unstick yourself

If you get stuck, try doing something else for a while. Something physical can help, such as going for a walk, doing a sport, dancing or singing.

The brain works in strange ways – sometimes, ideas come to you when you aren't trying to find them.

PAST POETRY
One of the world's oldest written stories is a poem called *The Epic of Gilgamesh*. It was written around 4,000 years ago.

Doorways for your imagination

Isabella Mead, from The Story Museum, Oxford, UK, has some helpful advice for how to use doorways in your stories. She says, "Imagine there's a door in front of you. How do you open the door? Where does the door lead? Who comes to greet you? Now, rather than a doorway, imagine it's a portal to another world. Books are full of portals – for example, Harry Potter rams his trolley into a wall. What will your portal be like?"

Write your autobiography

An autobiography is the story of a person's life, written by that person. Writing one can be a fun way to remember and record events that are important to you.

Here's how to get started.

Brainstorm first

Brainstorm the details you want to include. As a guide, make a big list of factual information – like where you were born and where you live – and then add major life events and favourite memories.

If you get stuck for ideas, scroll through old photos or ask a family member to tell you stories about your childhood.

Create an outline

An autobiography is usually written in chronological order, meaning that it would start when you were born and end with the present.

This means that your **outline** can be a timeline, with your oldest memories first. Look at your brainstorming notes and list your memories in chronological order.

Write your draft

Your autobiography should include full descriptions of your memories, and interesting details to help bring your story to life. You should write in the past tense.

As you write, you may see common themes. Many of the events that you've included might focus on your friendships, for example, or how you've handled change.

These common themes can help to connect different parts of your story. You could also include reflections about how you noticed these themes and what they mean to you.

Revise and share

Read and revise your writing until you're happy with the result. It may help to read it out loud to yourself.

As you read, ask yourself questions:

- Does this sound like me?
- Are there any extra words I don't need?
- Am I missing any key parts of my story?

After you make any adjustments, you could ask a family member or friend to read your autobiography too.

THAT'S WILD
Cave paintings found in Sulawesi, Indonesia, are believed to be at least 45,500 years old.

ASTONISHING ART

ARTY FOOD...

Art can be anything created to be beautiful or meaningful. It can also be created from all sorts of things, and food is one of them. Technically, you could eat all of these sculptures – but you probably shouldn't.

A sugary showstopper

Michelle Wibowo created a magnificent 0.76-metre-tall sculpture of London's Tower Bridge, spending more than 150 hours and 25 kilograms of sugar on it.

It was one of a number of pieces of art made from sugar or salt that were on show at an **exhibition** in London.

Dressed in dessert

Debbie Wingham, who is also known as the Countess of Confection, has created a dress out of an unusual material: cake.

This life-sized dress was crafted using 300 eggs, 25 boxes of Rice Krispie Treats and 13,000 baby marshmallows.

The project took months to complete because Wingham then decorated the dress using more than 25,000 edible flowers, carefully cut from rice paper by hand.

A sweet idea for the royal image

King Charles III has been recreated out of almost 3,000 Mars, Twix and Bounty bars.

Chocolatiers in Slough, UK, melted down 17 litres of Celebrations chocolate and shaped the goo into a sculpture of the king, wearing the uniform that he was set to wear at his coronation on 6 May 2023.

It took the team four weeks to make and a long time studying videos of the king to capture his looks.

Incredible bread art

A mother–daughter team has made a life-size **replica** of the *Star Wars* character Han Solo from an unlikely material: bread.

Visitors are amazed at the six-foot-tall sculpture, dubbed "Pan Solo" – using a **pun** on the French word for bread: *pain*, pronounced "pan".

The model, made entirely of dough, depicts a scene from a *Star Wars* film in which Solo is frozen. It took Hanalee Pervan, the head baker at One House Bakery in California, US, and her mum a month to build it.

A mouthwatering work of art

Using ingredients found in her kitchen, artist Kim Bainbridge has created a Dutch landscape made entirely from food.

Also known as a "foodscape", her creation used broccoli, berries, coffee, pasta and rosemary leaves. It took her 50 hours to make and was part of her final project for her art studies.

Bainbridge hates to waste food, so she ate the ingredients at the end of her delicious project.

...AND FOODIE ART

These are tempting treats that you *definitely* shouldn't try to taste.

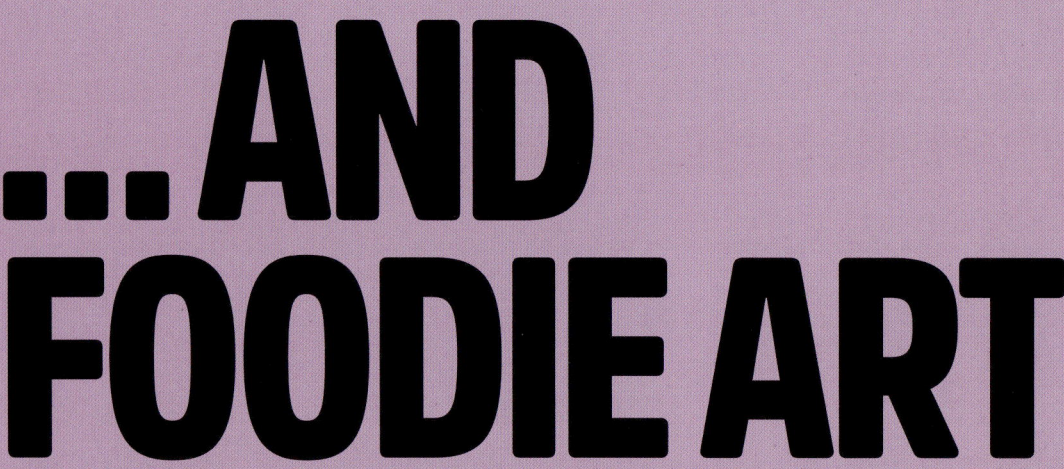

Fuzzy snacks, anyone?

Lucy Sparrow specialises in crafting things from felt that are designed to look like food.

In 2022, to celebrate Queen Elizabeth II's **platinum jubilee,** Lucy created a huge afternoon tea that featured cakes, biscuits and sandwiches.

In 2023, she opened a bagel shop in the seaside town of Montauk, US. Visitors could choose to buy "bagels" from a selection of 13 different kinds on display, and add "toppings" such as salt beef and pickles.

Water noodles

In 2022, a US hotel company called The Standard released a treat for people who love both swimming and Italian food. They could enjoy both at the same time – by bobbing along on a giant piece of "inflatable pasta".

The Standard sold these **quirky** designs as pool floats. Various delicious-looking pasta types were made available, including ravioli, tortellini and sheets of lasagne.

The floats came in fake pasta boxes with fun "nutritional facts" on the side. Lilos in the shape of macaroni cost pool-based pasta lovers $70 – about £55.

Fashion-flavoured bags

The famous fashion brand Balenciaga created a handbag that may seem more at home on a supermarket shelf. They teamed up with a US snack company called Lay's to create a bag that looked like a bag of crisps.

The bags were made from treated leather with a glossy finish. They were sold for a whopping $1,500. "Can y'all actually fill it to the top with chips?" asked one social media commenter.

Climbing a cake

Portuguese artist, Joana Vasconcelos, built this 12-metre-high wedding cake using china tiles as icing. People could tour the cake and even stand on top.

COOL CANVASES

Art isn't just hung in galleries: it can pop up anywhere. These **innovative** artists have chosen unusual places to show off their skills.

Tourists in Japan, look down

The streets of Japan are paved with beautifully decorated **manhole covers**. Decorating these common city features has been a tradition since the 1980s.

Artists take melted-down scrap metal and turn it into the right shape for the manhole. They then paint scenes from Japanese **culture** on it.

Designs include Mount Fuji, the highest mountain in Japan.

Artist's mega mountain art

In Villars-sur-Ollon, Switzerland, an artist known as Saype has created two huge pictures of children, using mountain slopes as his canvas.

The art was painted using environmentally friendly chalk and charcoal. They show a boy and a girl sketching the world around them as they see it. Each picture measures about 50 metres high.

Saype says that they show the importance of different perspectives.

Insect invasion takes over building

The Rijksmuseum in Amsterdam may be used to *displaying* canvases, but a group of artists used the whole building as a canvas in 2022.

Over 700 giant ants crawled through it as part of an exhibition called Crawly Creatures. It was intended to reflect people's changing attitudes towards animals like ants, snakes, spiders and toads.

Stunning street art

Although a lot of street art is created without the permission of its location's owners, many cities around the world celebrate it.

Pristina, Kosovo

The capital of Kosovo, Pristina, is making its public spaces more colourful by adding graffiti to walls and buildings.

Pristina is often called the "capital of concrete" because it has a lot of dull, grey buildings. During an art festival at the end of July 2023, more than 100 artists from 28 countries helped to brighten up the city with their street art.

Birmingham, UK

The High-Vis Festival, which takes place in the Digbeth area of Birmingham, UK, celebrates street culture, including breakdancing, graffiti, live music, skateboarding and street food.

In 2023, 50 artists painted colourful designs on walls and buildings in Digbeth, and the festival celebrated the 50th anniversary of hip-hop, a musical movement that began in New York, US.

Paris, France

The work of a famous street artist named Jace took over a building in a playful way. To gallery owners, the building's structure looked like the 1981 arcade game Donkey Kong – the game in which the character Mario first appeared.

The design features Mario, Donkey Kong and the princess, all painted in Jace's own style. The artist also altered the rewards that a player can collect into modern valuables, like a diamond ring and designer handbag.

FAKE CAKE

Want to try some foodie art of your own? Try a sponge cake made from a kitchen sponge.

What you need:

- thick cardboard (part of an old box would be fine)
- ruler
- felt-tip pen
- scissors
- one or more yellow sponges, ideally about three centimetres thick
- PVA glue and a spreader
- buttercream (or shaving foam)
- cake decorations, such as sprinkles

1. Gather all your materials together.

2. Draw triangles onto your cardboard, however big you want your cake slice to be.

5. Using the scissors, cut out your sponge triangles. Don't worry if they don't look perfect.

6. Sandwich a cardboard triangle between two sponge triangles using glue. Wash your spreader.

3. Cut out your triangles. The amount you need depends on how many slices of cake you want.

4. Draw around a triangle on the sponge. You'll need two sponge triangles per slice.

7. Paint buttercream or shaving foam over the cardboard strip, on top of the slice and down the back.

8. Decorate your slice or slices however you like – and admire your foodie artistry.

MYSTERY MODELS

Some artists are famous locally. Others are known all over the world. A few, however, choose to remain **anonymous**. Sometimes, they even make displaying their work into mysteries.

The mystery of the Minions

Scrap-metal sculptures of the **Minions** (characters from the film *Despicable Me*) kept popping up around the small Australian town of Warrack.

In the town of 70 residents, no one knew who was responsible. Cameras caught two people setting up a Minion, but neither was clear in the footage.

Their identities are still unknown. It remains a "good fun mystery", said one resident.

The mystery of the puzzling pole

A wildlife organisation in the UK was puzzled by a wooden pole. It looked similar to totem poles – beautifully carved monuments traditionally made by artists native to North America.

The nearly 2.5-metre-tall sculpture was installed overnight on a coastal path at a nature reserve. It was carved with the name "Perkunas", a **Baltic** god of thunder.

No artist was identified. A reserve manager said, "It's a totem mystery."

The mystery of the mailbox models

It was a special delivery for a couple from Michigan, US, who found that dolls had set up home in their mailbox.

The mailbox outside Don and Nancy Powell's house was a replica of their home. One day, Don opened it up to find that an unknown artist had added to it. Two dolls were sitting on a miniature sofa, with a note: "We've decided to live here," signed "Mary and Shelley".

Don quizzed his neighbours about the dolls, but they all denied any involvement. The mystery doll **donor** went on to sneak in wall art, a bed and a rug.

Nancy said, "It's very cute. I get a laugh out of it."

IS IT ART?

What do you think about these exhibits – are they art in your eyes?

Art disaster turns into opportunity

At a Miami art event, a woman accidentally knocked over a blue porcelain sculpture titled "Balloon Dog", which was worth over £34,000, before it shattered on the floor.

Art fans clamoured to buy the **shards**, though.

"I find value in it even when it's broken," said the collector Stephen Gamson.

Peckish student tucks into exhibit

A student was visiting an art museum when he felt his tummy rumble. Luckily, he spotted the perfect snack: a banana taped to the wall.

He plucked the banana from the tape and ate it, and then returned the skin to its spot. Unfortunately, it turned out that the banana was an exhibit. It had sold at **auction** for almost £100,000.

When he was told what had happened, the artist replied, "No problem." The museum replaced the skin with a fresh banana.

Real OR rubbish?

The art show of empty frames

An artist in Denmark is in big trouble.

An art museum gave him about £57,000 in paper money. He was hired to create art using the banknotes, to represent how much people earned in different countries.

Instead, the artist submitted blank canvases – and named his project "Take the Money and Run". The shocked staff of the museum demanded their cash back.

Is this story real or are we giving you a run for your money?*

* **Real!** A court ruled that the artist had to repay the money – but he could keep a fee for his "labour", since the museum still displayed the empty "artwork".

APPRECIATING ASTONISHING ART

There are many ways to appreciate different types of art and consider what the work might mean to you.

Visiting an art museum or gallery

Going to an art museum or gallery can be a fun activity to do with family and friends. For many people, though, viewing art can feel **intimidating** – or even boring – if you're not sure what the art is about.

If you're interested in exploring how to connect with paintings, sculptures and more, here are some steps to get you started.

Tate Modern, London, UK.

Choose a museum

Ask an adult to help you look at the websites of a few local galleries to see what types of art or special exhibits are on display.

Choose one showing something that interests you. If you love clothes, you might head to a fashion museum. If you enjoy taking photos, you might want to view a photography exhibit.

You can also visit museums online. Below are some suggestions that you might like to explore from home.

The British Museum

This museum in London, UK, offers an online collection featuring art and **artefacts** from around the world that date back as far back as two million years ago.

The Louvre

You can walk virtually around five galleries of this museum in Paris, France, to spot everything from paintings by artists like Rembrandt to an exhibit on the importance of dance.

The Metropolitan Museum of Art

The online time machine at this New York City museum features treasures such as an ancient bowl that sits on top of carved feet.

Exploring a museum

Take your time

When you're at the museum and a piece of art catches your eye, pause and spend some time really taking it in.

You can start by getting close to the artwork (without touching it) so that you can see details you might miss if you were viewing it online. If you're looking at a painting, for example, consider the texture on the surface and whether any brushstrokes are visible.

Then step back and look at the way the brushstrokes work together to create the image. You could try looking at it from a different angle or sketching it in a notebook. You might spot things that you didn't notice before.

Consider the meaning

Once you've absorbed the physical **aspects** of the work, try to find out more about what the artist intended it to mean. A volunteer at the museum may be available to talk to you about it. Free brochures may also provide information.

Part of the magic of art is how artists – especially those who might be from a different background or who lived thousands of years ago – can communicate meaning to others through their work.

Reflect on what you saw

Thinking about the meaning, subject, colours and setting of a piece of art can help you to better understand and appreciate artists and their work.

After you leave the museum, consider which pieces of art stay in your mind and why.

Ask yourself what the work means to you. For example, maybe the colours remind you of a place that's special to you, or perhaps it connects to emotions that you've been feeling.

Talk to a friend or adult who went with you, and ask them about their favourite pieces too.

FABULOUS FOOD

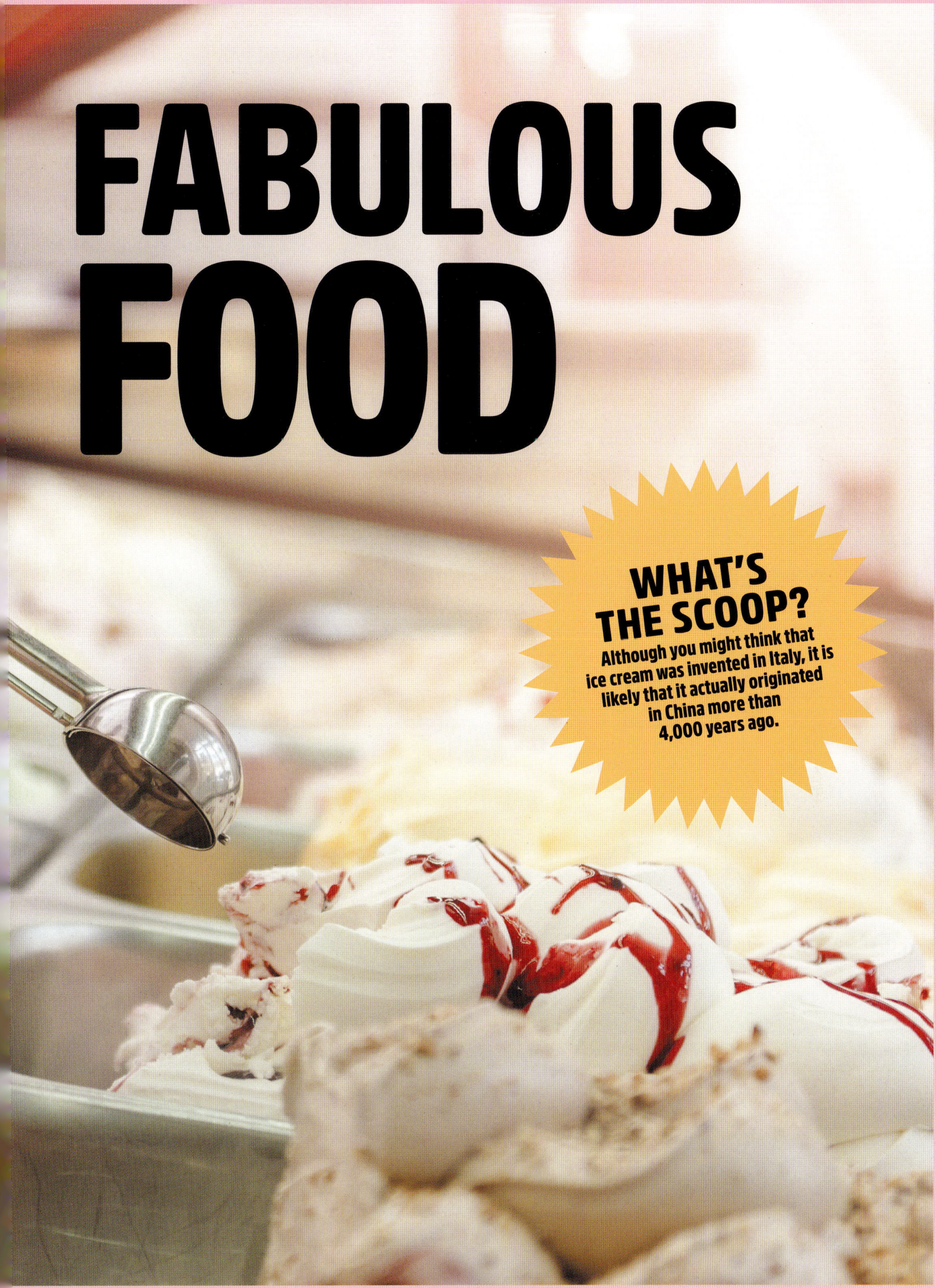

WHAT'S THE SCOOP?
Although you might think that ice cream was invented in Italy, it is likely that it actually originated in China more than 4,000 years ago.

SUPER-SIZED

Some clever cooks and shocked shoppers have taken the idea of "super-sized" food to the next level. How many hungry mouths do you think these feasts would feed?

Super sushi helps the homeless

In 2022 two chefs created a Guiness World Record-setting sushi roll – the widest in the world.

Nick DiGiovanni and Lynn Davis created the super-sized sushi using 227 kilograms of salmon, 900 kilograms of rice and millions of sesame seeds. The oversized fish dish was 2.16 metres wide and weighed the same as 45,000 regular-sized sushi rolls.

After the challenge, the giant sushi was donated to a shelter for homeless people.

Pizzeria delivers giant portions

Diners needed a big appetite before ordering from Big Mama's & Papa's Pizzeria in Los Angeles. Their speciality was the "Giant Sicilian", an enormous square pizza with each side measuring almost 140 centimetres. It was designed to separate into 200 square slices and feed up to 70 people.

The pizzeria said that they had to use a special oven extension and rotate the pizza to ensure that it cooked evenly. It took three people to get a huge pizza to a customer: one to make it and two to deliver it.

Cheese-tastic chips

To mark National Guacamole Day, Doritos pulled off a very cheesy stunt in Cheddar Gorge, UK, where cheddar cheese is made.

Using a helicopter, a giant tortilla chip and a bowl of melted cheese, they successfully completed a high-flying "cheese pull".

An impressive 120 kilograms of cheddar and mozzarella were melted in a pot, creating the perfect level of stretchiness for the cheese. The helicopter dipped the tortilla chip and then managed to stretch the cheese for nearly 15 metres without the string breaking.

When life gives you lemons ...

A bakery owner came across a lemon that was 22 centimetres long and weighed nearly 1.8 kilograms. Tammy Warren found the fantastic fruit at a greengrocer's stall in Chippenham, UK, and bought it for £5.

She then used it to make as many lemon-flavoured foods as she could. Her creations included a lemon drizzle cake, lemon syrup, lemon curd, lemon marmalade and fresh lemonade.

NACHO NIBBLES

If your taste buds are tingling after reading about a flying tortilla chip, ask an adult to help you make some nachos of your own.

Ingredients

- 1 tbsp olive oil
- 165 grams sweetcorn (cut from 1 large corn cob, tinned or frozen and thawed)
- 180 grams black beans (cooked or tinned), rinsed and drained
- 1 tsp herbs and spices you enjoy (such as paprika, oregano and chilli)
- 1 big bag tortilla chips (around 270 grams)
- 250 grams grated cheese
- 150 millilitres sour cream
- **zest** and juice of half a lime
- 1 avocado, chopped
- 2 tomatoes, chopped

Instructions

1. Preheat the oven to 200°C.
2. Heat the olive oil in a frying pan over a medium-high heat.
3. Add the corn and cook it for about five minutes, until it's tender and starting to brown.
4. Stir in the black beans with your herbs and spices, and heat them through.
5. Spread the tortilla chips evenly onto a baking tray or oven-proof dish.
6. Spoon the mixture of corn and black beans over the top, and then cover it with the grated cheese.
7. Bake the nachos for about five minutes, until the cheese is melted and bubbly.
8. While they cook, mix the sour cream with the lime zest and juice.
9. Using oven mitts, carefully remove the nachos from the oven.
10. Top with the avocado, tomato and lime sour cream.
11. Serve them immediately – and enjoy!

WARNING!
Always ask an adult to help you in the kitchen.

FUN FACT
The first nachos were created in 1940 by Ignacio "Nacho" Anaya, with just three ingredients: tortilla chips, cheese and spicy jalapeño peppers.

UNDERCOVER VEGETABLES

A sneaky type of ice cream

Almost everyone loves the taste of chocolate ice cream, but fewer are keen on beetroot and parsnip. To get their children to eat more veg, three dads created a range of ice cream recipes that contain hidden vegetables.

Each flavour has regular ice cream ingredients – sugar and milk – plus an extra scoop of secret vegetable. The chocolate contains beetroot, vanilla is packed with parsnips and the strawberry smuggles in carrots.

The inventors say that you can't taste the vegetables but the ice cream still gets the goodies into reluctant vegetable eaters.

JUST JOKING
What did the vegetable lover campaign for? A celery increase and world peas!

A musical carrot creation

Boris Sichon has spent his musical career crafting instruments out of unlikely objects. He now has a fabulous collection of more than 600.

One of his most unusual is normally found in recipes rather than orchestras: a recorder carved out of a carrot.

Artist sculpts fish out of broccoli

A sculpture of a leaping fish made from a stalk of broccoli was created in Japan.

The sculptor is a chef and artist who goes by the name Gaku. He has also made a rabbit out of an avocado, a flower from a watermelon and a shrimp from a carrot.

He spent three hours creating the broccoli fish, carving each individual scale in detail.

His skills are a Japanese technique called *mukimono*, which involves carving fruits and vegetables into amazing designs.

Examples of *mukimono* on display.

FANTASTICAL FLAVOURS

Candy for condiment lovers

A popular sweets brand has developed a **controversial** new flavour. For National Mustard Day on 5 August 2023, French's Mustard worked with SKITTLES to create French's Mustard SKITTLES.

They said that the "unique summer treat" combined the candy's chewy texture with French's "tangy" taste. The limited-edition flavour sparked some strong reactions.

"I'd love to try these!" said one mustard lover on social media.

Another person wrote, "This is absolutely disgusting, rancid, and wrong. Hey @Skittles, how can I get them?"

The sweet without a flavour

When a new type of sweet landed on Japanese shelves, it proved controversial. That's because it wasn't sweet – in fact, it had no flavour at all.

The product, named "Flavourless (?) Candy", was made for people who wanted to relieve a dry mouth but didn't want a sugar rush.

One consumer described it as being like "ice that is not cold".

Strawberry or pineapple?

A Dutch fruit breeder, Hans de Jongh, developed pineberries, a cross between red European strawberries and white South American strawberries. They tasted a bit like pineapple.

Heinz also created some extraordinary ice cream: ketchup flavour!

Grab a cone – or a slice?

Ice cream company Van Leeuwen released an original flavour in 2022: pizza-inspired ice cream. The flavour was made with mozzarella and cream cheese, swirls of tomato jam and basil crust cookies.

Van Leeuwen had gone down this aisle before, releasing a macaroni and cheese ice cream the previous year as part of what the company called "flavours that you would never expect to love".

A SWEET AND SAVOURY SALAD

Follow these instructions for a tasty tomato and peach Caprese salad.

Ingredients

- 350 to 450 grams cherry tomatoes
- 2 ripe peaches
- 125 grams fresh mozzarella ball
- freshly picked basil leaves
- 2 tbsp white balsamic vinegar
- 1 tbsp freshly squeezed lemon juice
- 60 millilitres olive oil
- salt and pepper

Instructions

1. On a cutting board, use a knife to slice each cherry tomato into two halves.
2. Cut the peaches in half and remove the stones.
3. Cut the peach halves into slices.
4. Tear the ball of mozzarella into small pieces.
5. Arrange the tomatoes, peaches, mozzarella and basil together in a large serving bowl. You can keep the salad refrigerated until you're ready to serve it.
6. In a small bowl, whisk together the white balsamic vinegar, lemon juice and olive oil. Season the dressing to taste with salt and pepper.
7. Drizzle the dressing over the salad just before serving.

WARNING! Always ask an adult to help you in the kitchen.

DID YOU KNOW? Caprese salad comes from the island of Capri. Capri is a beautiful island off the coast of Italy and is popular with tourists.

OUT AND ABOUT

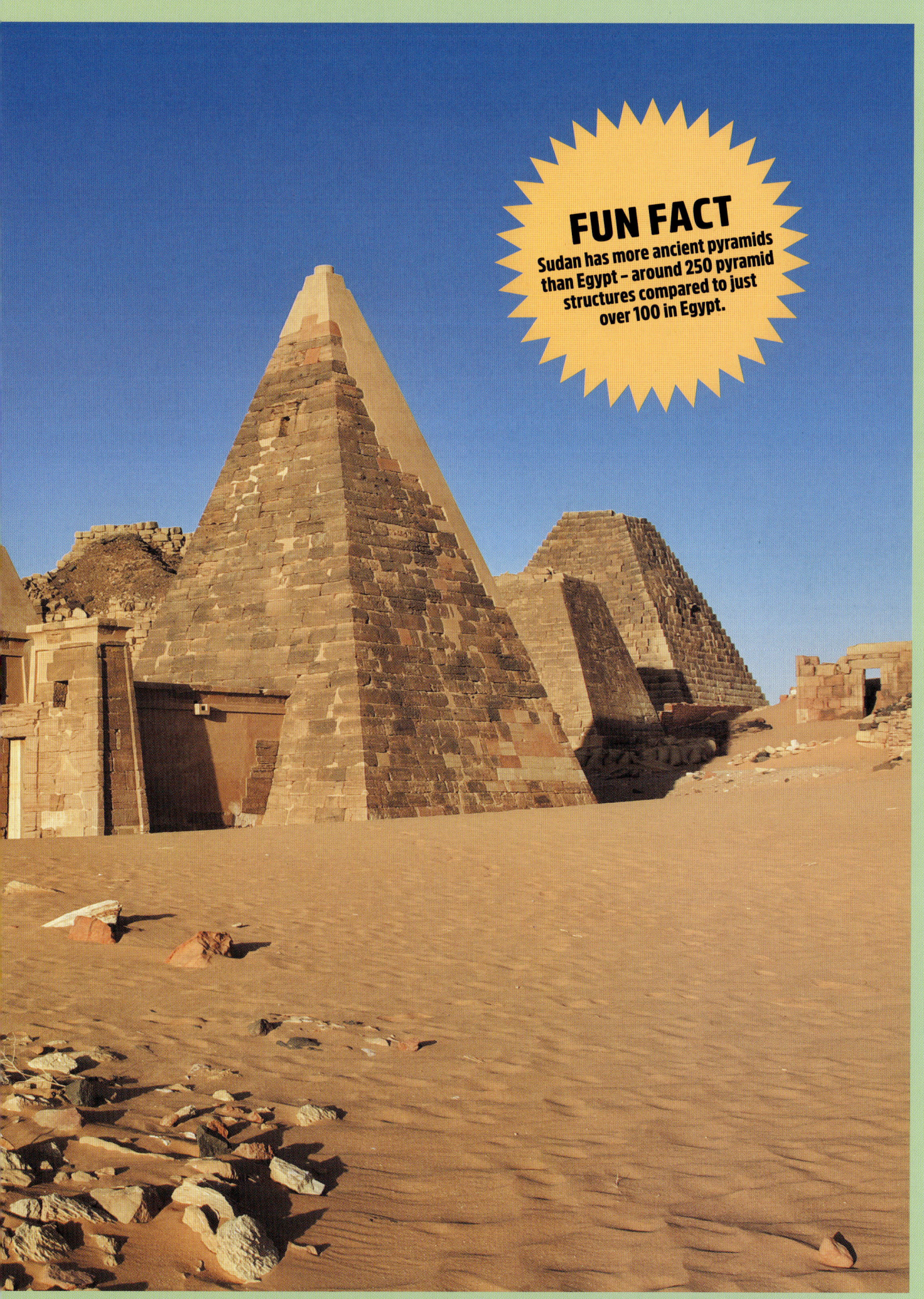

FUN FACT
Sudan has more ancient pyramids than Egypt – around 250 pyramid structures compared to just over 100 in Egypt.

VACATION CREATIONS

The deepest sleep in the world

If visitors to Eryri (Snowdonia) National Park in Wales are looking for some time to themselves, they only need to go underground to the world's deepest overnight accommodation.

Visitors can stay more than 400 metres underground in a high-class cave room or a heated log cabin. These luxury lodgings are in a cavern that was once part of a slate mine.

The journey, down miners' stairs and over very old bridges, is apparently worth it. Guests have described their nights underground as the "best sleep of their lives".

PLEASE DO NOT DISTURB

ZZZZZZZ

The aeroplane holiday home

On top of a cliff on the island of Bali, Indonesia, an aeroplane has been turned into a two-bedroom holiday home with a swimming pool.

Converting the Boeing 737 aeroplane into a luxury villa was extremely complicated. The plane had to be taken apart so that it could be carried by road to the cliff-top location, which involved two cranes and a police escort.

All that effort has been reflected in the price. A one-night stay in this flight of fancy would cost more than £5,800.

Real OR rubbish?

Living like an ogre

Have you ever wanted to live the life of an ogre in your very own swamp? A real-life recreation of Shrek's home made that a reality.

In true Shrek style, this isolated Scottish property didn't have a proper shower, but instead a mud bath, with a pond for rinsing off afterwards. It also came with a donkey to keep the inhabitant company.

Is this story real or have we created a fairytale fantasy?*

***Rubbish!** The property did exist, but didn't require guests to live their lives like ogres. It was available for someone to stay in as a one-off experience, aiming to raise money for charity.

TERRIBLE TOURISM

People travel the world for all sorts of reasons: fantastic food, amazing hotels, stunning scenery – the list goes on and on. Some supposed tourist destinations seem simply bizarre, though.

The puddle covered a section of the car park.

Tourists flood to see ... a big puddle

A giant puddle in the car park of a restaurant in Minnesota, US, became a tourist attraction.

Minnesota is famous for its lakes, but this one – known jokingly as Lake Chipotle – was a bit different. The "lake" covered most of the car park at a restaurant called Chipotle Mexican Grill.

The big puddle drew sightseers and even the occasional paddle boarder, and was given its own website. One restaurant worker claimed that on really cold days, he put on his ice skates to get across it.

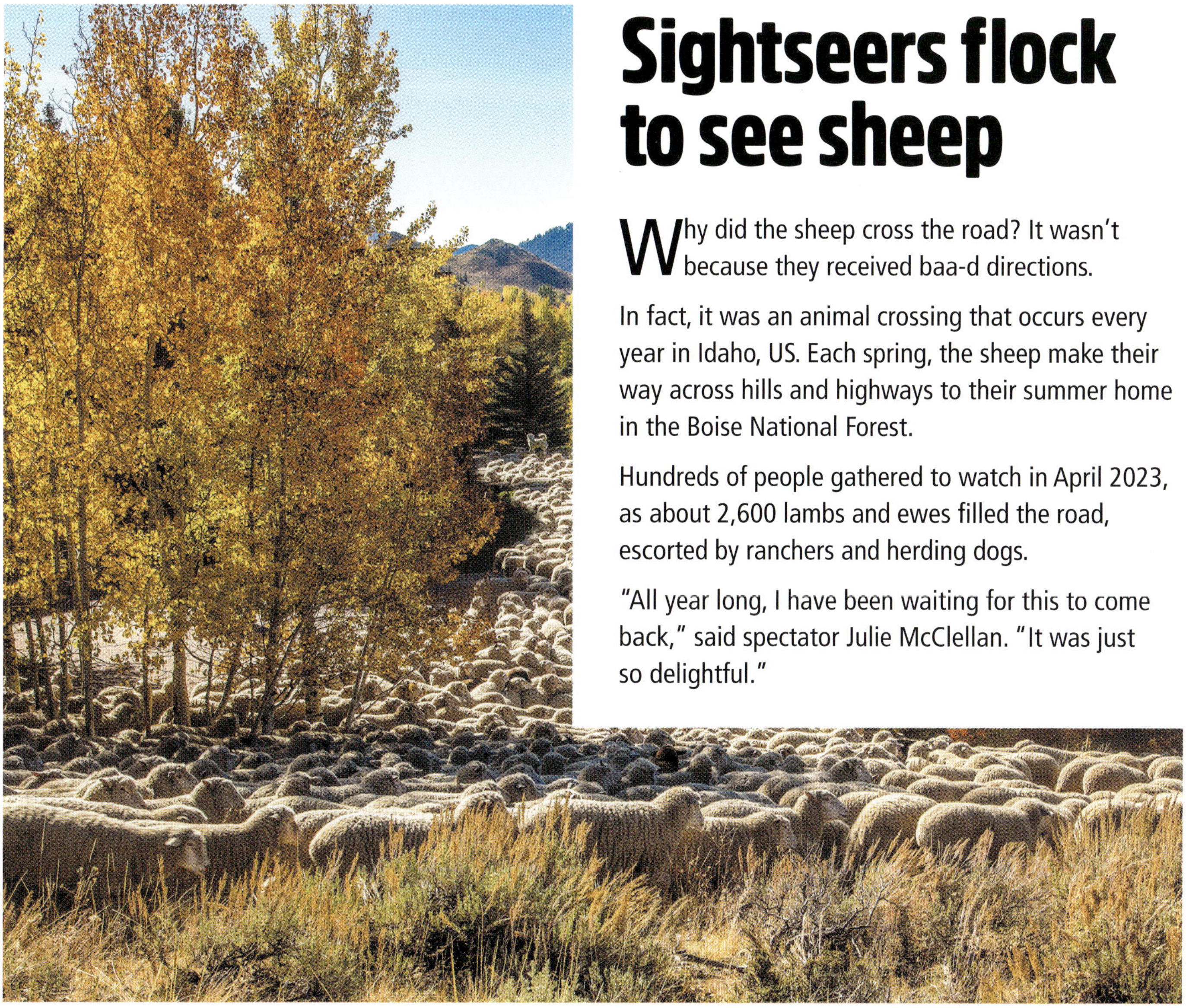

Sightseers flock to see sheep

Why did the sheep cross the road? It wasn't because they received baa-d directions.

In fact, it was an animal crossing that occurs every year in Idaho, US. Each spring, the sheep make their way across hills and highways to their summer home in the Boise National Forest.

Hundreds of people gathered to watch in April 2023, as about 2,600 lambs and ewes filled the road, escorted by ranchers and herding dogs.

"All year long, I have been waiting for this to come back," said spectator Julie McClellan. "It was just so delightful."

Cat beats castle in tourist vote

The King of Kaszubska Street, in the Polish city of Szczecin, might not have had a crown – but he strolled around as if he owned the place. This "king" was a tubby black-and-white cat by the name of Gacek, which translates as "long-eared bat".

Gacek clawed his way to the top as the city's most popular tourist attraction after he was filmed by a local news station. The video went viral on social media, and visitors kept giving him five stars in reviews.

Gacek soon achieved a higher rating than the city's 12th century castle, and tourists visited the town especially to see him. He lived on the street, though, and could be grumpy when woken – so his fans weren't always welcome.

ODD JOBS

People get paid for all kinds of weird and wonderful work. Do any of these jobs appeal to you?

A screaming success

Benjamin Meehan, a full-time professional rollercoaster rider, spent every weekend at theme parks around the US, earning money by filming his rides and posting them on YouTube.

Meehan has visited every big theme park in the country, but his favourite is Universal Studios, Florida, US, which is just two hours from his home. Back at his house, Meehan works on his YouTube content – which is mostly videos of high-speed rides to the sound of people screaming.

Call for a Chief of Cheer

Cosying up with some hot cocoa and a film was all in a day's work for one lucky person, whose job involved watching a Christmas-themed film every day for a month.

The "Chief of Cheer" was hired by CableTV.com to express opinions about festive films. They got free access to streaming services plus around £80 per film watched.

"Trust us, it sounds easier than it is," said a CableTV.com spokesperson. They added that the successful applicant would "have to supply your own hot chocolate and gingerbread."

Seeking a chief penguin officer

The tour operator Antarctica21 advertised a rather unusual position: chief flying penguin officer (CFPO). To mark the 20th anniversary of its first expedition, the company selected one lucky candidate for a free week-long trip to Antarctica.

The CFPO's only duties were to explore and "share in our passion for the continent," the company said. Applicants simply had to be at least 18 years old and answer three questions about penguins.

Where do I sign up?

The Royal Swan Marker

Every July, the Royal Swan Marker and a team of Swan Uppers row along the River Thames, UK, shouting "All up!" when they see a family of mute swans and their **cygnets**.

The birds, which (like all swans) are owned by the UK's **monarch**, are weighed, measured and checked for any injuries.

When David Barber, the current Swan Marker, was interviewed for the job in 1993, he suggested that more should be done to protect the beautiful birds.

"The Palace liked the idea and the Queen appointed me," he said.

Just the job for fans of Uno

The toy company Mattel hired a chief Uno player to test out its new Uno Quatro family game. Similar to the original Uno game, Uno Quatro is a bit like Connect 4 and involves getting four coloured or numbered chips in a row.

The job advert for the role said that the lucky candidate could earn more than £3,500 per week for four weeks of playing the game.

Real OR rubbish?

Cheese lovers' dreamy job

Have you heard the saying that eating cheese before bed gives you nightmares? Researchers put that theory to the test.

Five lucky people were paid £800 to tuck into cheese before they snoozed. For three months, each cheese tester had to take notes about their dreams, how they slept and how they felt during the day.

So, is this a "grate" story – and a "brie-lliant" experiment – or is it as full of holes as Swiss cheese?*

*Real! Yes, you "feta" believe it! A company called Sleep Junkie really did test the theory that chomping on cheese before sleep gives people bad dreams.

WHAT A WAY TO LIVE!

These quirky creatives made unusual choices about their homes.

Mr Doodle decorates his home

Imagine buying a mansion and then drawing all over the walls. Artist Sam Cox – known as Mr Doodle – did just that. He decorated his six-bedroom house in Kent, UK, with black, cartoon-like drawings.

Cox bought the house in 2019 after selling his art, and then spent up to 12 hours a day doodling away. He drew on the bath, the bed and even the toilet. The talented artist said that completing the house was "just the beginning of my childhood dream to doodle the planet".

Artist moves into a rubbish skip

An artist in South East London, UK, lived in a converted **skip** for one year to highlight the **cost-of-living crisis**.

Artist Harrison Marshall decided to live in the cramped skip because the cost of renting a flat or room in the area "had kind of gone crazy".

However, he did fit a roof to keep out the rain. The Skip House, as it was known, became part of Skip Gallery, a project aimed at helping artists early on in their careers.

Home not-so-sweet home

Carmen Croxall loved Christmas so much that she spent two weeks transforming the front of her home into a giant gingerbread house.

However, even though it was covered in tasty treats, including biscuit window sills, a candy cane door and lollipop trees, none of it could be eaten. Croxall, who lives in Exeter, UK, decorated her delicious-looking house using mostly recycled materials, such as old milk cartons.

"I'm really happy with how it looks," she said at the time, "but now that it's done, I'm already thinking about what I can do next."

FUNNY FESTIVALS

Many festivals celebrate cultural, religious and historical events. Some of them are inspired by more unusual things. Which of these do you think looks most fun?

Silent rocking

The Air Guitar World Championships are part of the Oulu August Festivals in Finland. Contestants compete to be the air guitar champion, silently rocking solos for two one-minute rounds.

Chasing cheese

The cheese-rolling festival takes place every year at Coopers Hill in Brockworth, Gloucestershire, UK. The world-famous event attracts both locals and daredevils from around the globe and involves chasing a four-kilogram **wheel** of cheese down a hill.

Beach kite festival takes off

Thousands of kite fans gather in Lancashire, UK, for the annual St Anne's Kite Festival.

Teams from the UK, Germany, India, Ireland and Norway take spectacular large kites to the event at St Anne's beach to show off their skills.

Visitors are invited to bring their own as well. The kites that take to the skies often include colourful models of dragons, horses, teddy bears and sea creatures.

A spud-tacula street party

In 2023, Chepstow, a town in Wales, announced plans to start holding potato-themed festivals. The decision was inspired by a spud-like artwork that was unveiled earlier in the year.

The sculpture, which cost £6,000, was supposed to look like a pebble. Locals, however, thought that it looked more like a baked potato wrapped in foil.

Events at the festival included a potato-sack race, a home-grown potato competition and potato-cooking demonstrations.

A German fruitcake parade

Residents of the German city of Dresden love **stollen** so much that it's celebrated in an annual parade before Christmas.

In the weeks before "Stollenfest", bakeries around Dresden produce hundreds of batches of individual stollen, which are then stuck together with butter and sugar to make one giant cake.

The huge stollen is carried through the city and cut into pieces for locals and visitors to enjoy.

HIGH IN THE SKY

Feeling inspired by those festivals? You could celebrate potatoes, cheese, buns or cake with a really good meal. If you're keen on kites, though, you could try out this activity with a friend.

1. Choose a kite

If you're a beginner, consider choosing a kite that's easier to handle and flies more steadily: a large, light kite, with a classic triangle or diamond shape and a long tail.

2. Find a spot

Scope out a large open space for flying, like a field or beach. It's important to be away from big trees or power lines so that the kite won't get stuck. It's also better if there aren't too many people around.

3. Check the wind

A smooth, steady wind without a lot of big gusts is ideal for kite flying. Step outside and feel for the wind. If you notice a breeze on your face, there's probably enough wind to fly a kite.

4. Launch the kite

Stand with your back to the wind. Ask your friend to face the wind and hold the kite up over their head, while you back up and unravel about 30 metres of the kite's string.

Signal your friend to let go. Quickly roll in the kite's line or jog in the other direction. This should push the kite into the air.

5. Fly it high

As long as the kite's line is **taut**, you can keep letting out more string. If the line **slackens**, you should reel in your string to keep the kite up.

Once you're ready to bring your kite down, reel the string back in until the kite is low enough to grab.

RARE RESTAURANTS

Fantastical flavours can be found at these extraordinary eateries.

Lunch that's truly out of this world

Food fans are often keen to travel around the globe to try new foods and flavours. Very soon, this passion could take people on a brand new journey to taste some very fine dining – on the edge of space.

A special lunch, which will cost an estimated £150,000, will be offered to guests in a stratospheric balloon 15 miles above Earth.

Each flight will have just six passengers on board, who will tuck into the delicious French food and admire views that, until now, have been seen only by astronauts.

Food from the future

Food fans have been flocking to a futuristic new restaurant that floats in a **fjord** in Rosendal, Norway.

The menu at Iris has 18 courses, all inspired by the sea and designed to protect the environment. Diners sit inside the Salmon Eye, a steel-plated art installation, for six hours while eating and watching a film about food waste.

Dinner costs more than £230 per person, and it's booked up months in advance.

Grandmothers cook for a crowd

Eating at Enoteca Maria is like having dinner at grandma's house, thanks to the New York restaurant's "**nonnas** of the world".

Owner Joe Scaravella hired Italian grandmothers (knows as nonnas in Italian) to make meals from his childhood. He then opened the kitchen to women from across the globe – Japanese, Indian, Brazilian and more – to cook dishes from their own cultures.

Every day, diners clap for the cooks. "It's like a family feeling," said nonna Yumi Komatsudaira.

A weird and wonderful dinner

A restaurant called Alchemist, in Copenhagen, Denmark, offers some very unusual food.

The menu is made up of 50 courses, including a freeze-dried butterfly, "space bread", a dish that resembles a human eye and a "tongue kiss" – a dish with food that is licked off a very life-like tongue. The price is around £567 per person.

Diners sit under a giant dome with light projections of jellyfish swimming around the ceiling. After their long, expensive meal, they are taken to a giant ball pit and encouraged to jump in.

Diners can choose "tongue kiss" from the menu.

SPECTACULAR

STAY COOL
In ice hockey, the pucks (the disc that players hit with their sticks) are frozen so that they don't bounce too much during the game.

SPORTS

DOWN AND DIRTY

There are some super but surprising sports out there. These ones cover their competitors in all kinds of gloop.

Slippery wrestlers get the gravy

Fans of roast dinners might have had more than their fill when they gathered in Rossendale, UK, for the 2023 World Gravy Wrestling Championships. Hundreds of spectators came to watch competitors battle it out in two-minute matches in a slimy, gravy-filled pool.

One of the wrestlers, Tommy Jupiter, said, "My opponent's eyes and ears were full of gravy, but we got through it." Judges awarded points for the wrestling, as well as how entertaining the matches were.

Bog snorkellers dive in

At the World **Bog** Snorkelling Championships, competitors must battle their way through cold and muddy waters.

The wacky event takes place each year at the end of August, near the town of Llanwrtyd Wells in Wales. There are prizes in adult, junior and international categories.

In the unusual sport, competitors have to snorkel along a boggy channel in the fastest time they can. The channel is a shallow, muddy trench cut through a wetland area. Every entrant wears a snorkel, mask and flippers, and has to complete two lengths of the 60-metre bog.

The basic rules are simple:

• Proper swimming strokes are not allowed, just a doggy-paddle technique.

• Arms must stay at or below the **waterline**.

• Faces must stay underwater – meaning that the snorkel is vital.

The contest has a juniors category as well as one for adults. Do you think you could become a boggy beginner?

Sporting smush

The annual Tomatina Festival in Spain is like an ultimate battle for glory: a town-wide food fight. For one day, the streets of the town of Buñol become a battleground, using overripe tomatoes that would otherwise be thrown away.

The food fight was inspired by one held by local kids in 1945, but it has now become a major event that draws tourists to the town.

In 2023, more than 15,000 people hurled 120,000 kilograms of tomatoes at one another. Participants wore goggles to protect their eyes from flying fruit, then hit the showers after the contest ended.

FAST AND SLOW

Taking toy horses for a ride

In Seinäjoki, Finland, people with an unusual pastime strutted their stuff at the Hobby Horse Championships.

Competitors were there to "ride" a hobby horse – a stuffed toy horse head on a stick – in events real horses compete in, such as show jumping and western riding. In show jumping, contestants leapt over 1.5-metre-tall fences while balancing the hobby horse between their legs.

"It's both hilarious and fascinating to watch," one observer wrote.

Racing dinos tear up the track

The Emerald Downs racetrack in Washington, US, typically hosts competitions for horses. For one weekend each summer, though, it's the site of the T. Rex World Championships.

In 2023, more than 200 people dressed in inflatable dinosaur costumes and ran a 100-metre dash. It was a close finish, with two T. rexes crossing the finish line in approximately nine seconds.

The subtle art of doing nothing

Do you think you could beat the record?

A group of people took part in an unusual competition in Seoul, South Korea. Their task? To sit around without any distractions, including conversation and food.

Seoul hosts the contest every year to show that "doing nothing is also valuable". Competitors must remain as zoned-out as possible, and anyone who laughs or dozes off is disqualified.

Settling down for a big win

The village of Brenza in Montenegro has an even more extreme low-energy contest. Each year, contestants compete hard for the title of "laziest citizen".

The rules state that the contestants must lie down and do nothing. Standing – or even sitting – results in instant disqualification. They are, however, allowed a 10-minute toilet break every eight hours.

DOUBLING UP

These sporting achievements are doubly impressive – because they're each "double" sports (or more).

A hula-spinning star

If you've ever tried hula-hooping, you'll know it takes some practice. A **performance artist** called Mariam Olayiwola has managed to spin up to 25 hoops – while on stilts.

Olayiwola started focusing on her hula-hooping expertise only after she suffered an accident. In 2019, she was struck by a car and broke her leg.

She had surgery on it and, during the six weeks when she wore a cast, decided to follow her passions: she became a full-time athletic performance artist.

On her hands and in her toes

Orissa Kelly is an amazing athlete, doubling up for not one but two impressive performances.

She can shoot arrows – not by using her arms and hands, but with her feet. She can also **manipulate** other objects with her toes, including batons that she can spin in time.

Kelly is a professional acrobat. She performs daring routines in which she demonstrates her incredible tricks. She has worked on the set of the film *Wonder Woman*, doing stunts for other actors, and even performed in front of Queen Elizabeth II.

Would you pick a pickleball?

The first Scottish national pickleball championship took place in Glasgow in the summer of 2023.

Pickleball combines badminton, ping pong and tennis, and has become popular in recent years. Fans include tennis coach Judy Murray, mother of tennis star Andy Murray. She describes it as "fun, sociable, accessible and very doable".

CAUGHT
IN THE ACT

Some matches cause pride and joy, some cause disappointment. However, these US sports contributions have proved nothing short of embarrassing.

Delivering a time-out

A US college basketball game was interrupted when a man walked onto the court with a food delivery. He seemed to be searching for the person who had ordered the meal.

The man nearly ran into one of the players before a referee stopped the game. The teams laughed it off, and university officials later concluded that the incident was a **prank**.

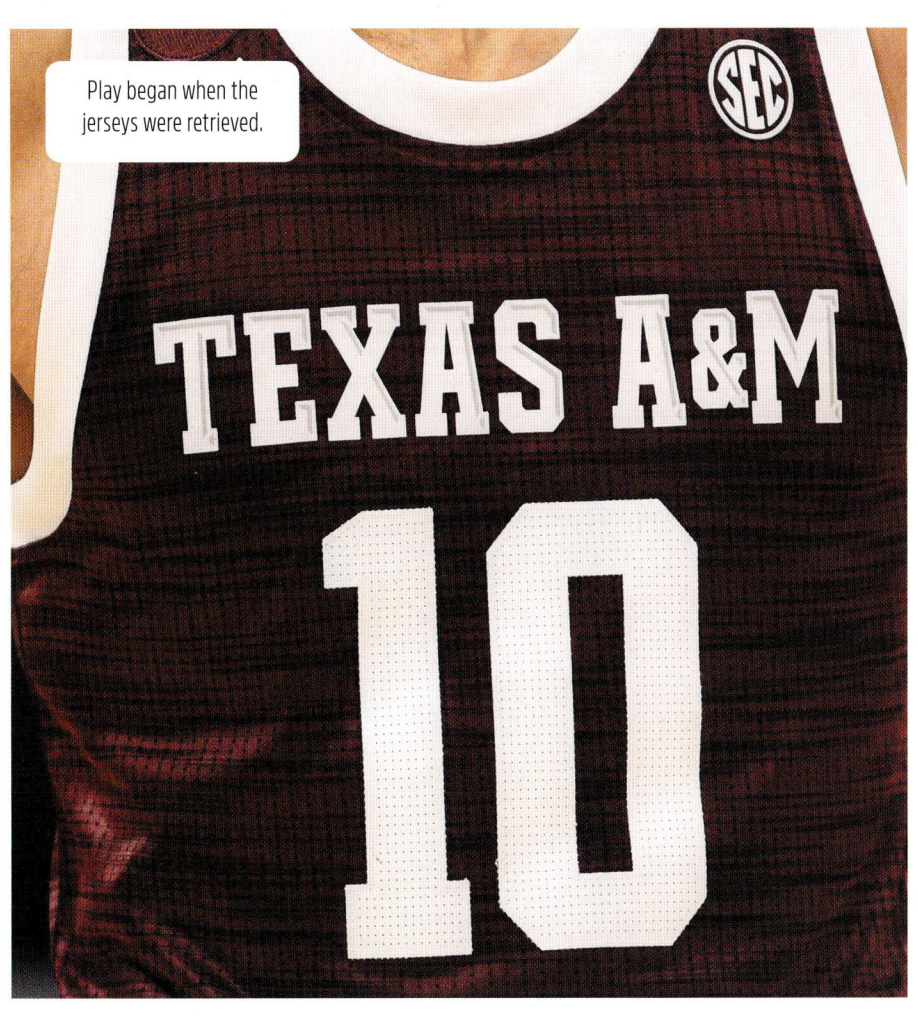

Play began when the jerseys were retrieved.

A full-court case of forgetfulness

In Texas, US, another basketball game was delayed when one team, the Texas A&M Aggies, forgot to bring their jerseys. Head coach Buzz Williams explained that the garments had been hanging in a hotel room and never made it onto the bus.

Their competition, the University of Florida, was awarded a free throw for the Aggies' "technical foul", while the Texans rushed to **retrieve** their uniforms. The Aggies came back – properly clothed – and won 66–63.

Real OR rubbish?

Secret hockey socks

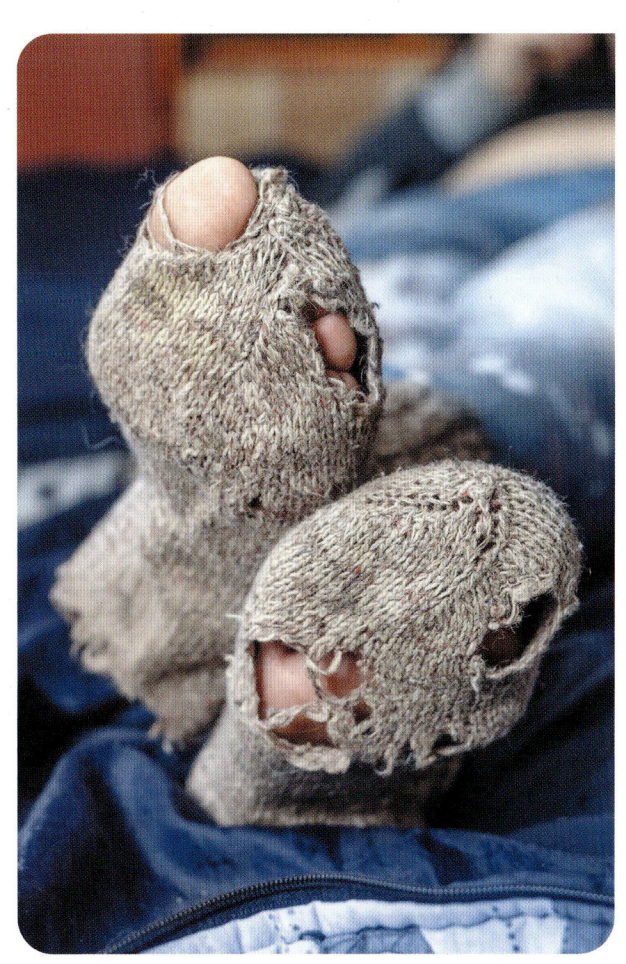

Connor McDavid, captain of a US ice hockey team called the Edmonton Oilers, was humiliated when a fellow player revealed that McDavid has worn the same pair of socks during every game of his eight-year career.

McDavid's toes stuck out through large holes, his teammate said, but he loved the grip that he got from that particular pair and insisted they brought him luck.

Is this story real or a big, stinky lie?*

***Rubbish!** McDavid did wear the same socks for every game, but he wasn't embarrassed when the truth came out. In fact, it was he who revealed his smelly **superstition**.

SPIRITED SUPPORT

Sports can be a great way to come together – whether you're playing them or simply watching them at home. You could show your team spirit by organising a fun match-day party.

Choose a match

Ask an adult to help you look for a **televised** match or game that everyone will enjoy. Some games may be more exciting than others to watch as a group. For instance, hosting a match-day party might be most fun if your team is competing in a cup final or playing against its top rival.

Plan the menu

As the host of the party, you can decide what kind of food to serve.

You could provide a main course, such as pizza, and then ask guests to bring other snacks and sweets. You could decide to skip a main course and just serve plenty of snacks.

Have water and other drinks on hand.

DID YOU KNOW?
The first ever FIFA World Cup was held in Uruguay in 1930.

Invite friends

Make a list of who you want to invite and ask an adult to help you get in touch with them. If your family wants to watch together, you could invite another family to join you.

Invite everyone to arrive about half an hour before the match starts. That way, people can chat and enjoy some food before the game begins.

Set the mood

Homemade decorations can make the area around your TV feel spirited. You could make paper chains in your team's colours or hang banners with messages on them around the room. You could suggest that your guests wear their team's colours, too.

Then make sure that everyone's comfortable – and wait for the match to begin.

FINDING YOUR PASSION

Discovering that you have a passion for a sport or hobby not only brings you joy – it can also boost your **self-esteem** and make you more confident.

Try a new activity

Try something new, like auditioning for the school play, doing a junior parkrun or visiting an art gallery.

You could also write a list of things you enjoy, such as camping, exploring woods and climbing trees. See if there's a thread that connects them, such as exploring the outdoors.

Get inspired

Join a club to get inspired by other people who share your interests. You may be aware of clubs, teams and hobby centres near you, or you could ask at school or your local library for ideas.

Try indoor rock climbing

This adventurous activity involves ascending an imitation rock wall, which has grips and foot holds all the way up. On large walls, climbers are supported by a rope.

Many indoor climbing gyms also feature bouldering walls, which are smaller and don't require a rope. They're great for beginners.

TOP TIPS

• Find your closest special rock-climbing gym or enquire about local recreation centres and schools that have climbing programmes.

• Make sure that you listen carefully to your climbing instructor. They'll have advice about everything, from equipment and safety to the routes that you'll most enjoy.

• Think about your goals on each trip: give yourself a realistic height to reach. Don't be dismayed if you don't reach it straight away – you can always come back and try again.

Give roller skating a go

Roller skating is good exercise, builds balance and can improve your mental focus. You can skate around a roller rink to music or roll through a local park enjoying the outdoors.

TOP TIPS

- You can often borrow equipment from a roller rink while you're there. Make sure that you strap on a helmet, elbow pads and knee pads for safety.

- Start simply. Practise standing on your skates. Sit down and stand up a few times, testing your balance.

- Get ready to roll. Begin by walking on your skates, keeping your toes turned outwards.

- As you walk, your wheels will start to glide. Allow yourself to glide slowly, keeping your knees bent.

Boost your wellbeing with a walk

According to experts, walking isn't just good for your physical health. It can also clear your mind, sharpen your senses and lift your mood.

TOP TIPS

- If your journey takes you through fields or a park, notice the nature around you. You could make a game out of trying to spot a different bird or insect every day.

- Walking along pavements is a chance to get to know your neighbourhood better.

- Enjoy quality time by walking with friends or family. This is a great opportunity to catch up and talk about your day.

- Keep a walk journal.

Bring out the board games

Board games are a great way to relax and have fun. There are competitive games, **collaborative** games and even one-person games.

There are games for all kinds of occasions: party games that make you laugh so much it hurts, strategic games for deep thinking, nail-biting games – and everything in between.

TOP TIPS

- If you're playing with other people, choose your players and find a time that works for everyone.
- Pick board games that suit you and your fellow players.
- Make things comfortable with a steady table and cosy cushions to sit on.
- Get snacks and drinks ready in case people need a break.
- Keep the peace by making sure that everyone knows the rules of the game.

Just join in

Whether you love music, sports, art or reading, there are lots of ways to join in group activities – like trying out a drama club or sports team. As well as meeting people who share the same interests as you, getting involved helps you to discover skills you may not know you have.

TOP TIPS

- You stay motivated. Being part of a team means relying on each other. This makes it easier to stick at a sport, even when you lose.

- You can make friends. Spending lots of time together and building trust helps you to connect with others.

- Your confidence builds. Learning new skills together and developing them with support can boost your confidence.

WONDERFUL WELLBEING

SMILE AWAY
Scientists have proved that smiling really does make you happy. When you smile, your brain releases chemicals that make you feel more positive and less stressed.

GETTING A GREAT START

Every good day starts with a good morning. Are you a ray of sunshine or a bit of a grump first thing in the morning? With these simple tips, you can start your day in a great mood.

Your thoughts affect your feelings

There are lots of things that can affect how you feel at the start of a day, such as how well you slept or how the people around you are behaving. Some of these things are out of your hands but others are things you can control, like your thoughts.

Young people's counsellor Angela McMillan explains that feelings are an emotional response to thoughts. She says, "Shifting what you focus your attention on can have an impact on how you feel."

For example, if you have a thought like "I don't want to do the maths test today", it could prompt you to feel anxious. Then what you do – your behaviour – is influenced by your thoughts and feelings. Thoughts of the maths test could mean that you're slow to get ready for school.

Before you even open your eyes or get out of bed, try naming three things that you're looking forward to that day. You'll be more likely to start out in a positive frame of mind.

Before you go out of the door

Focus on what you're doing. If you're brushing your teeth, for example, focus on watching your reflection in the mirror, or pay attention to cleaning each tooth.

As you're getting dressed, think of three things you're grateful for right now. That could be a new bag, or perhaps it's sunny outside, or maybe you're eating your favourite cereal.

While you're eating breakfast, boost your good mood by thinking of something kind that you can do today.

If you don't have a lot of time in the morning, you could try chef Jamie Oliver's advice. He says, "Short on time? Try blitzing up some fruit and veg with oats for a quick smoothie."

DID YOU KNOW? The word "breakfast" means to break your fast since the night before.

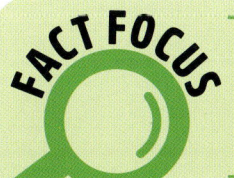 FACT FOCUS — Why bother with breakfast?

Breakfast is a very important meal: it gives your energy a real boost. There are lots of studies that show the benefits that breakfast has on your attention, memory and organising skills. This is because breakfast fuels your body and feeds your brain.

SUCCEEDING AT SCHOOL

School can be tough, but it can also bring out your best. Consider these ideas to help you get the most out of it.

Keep an open mind

To be positive learners, we all need to keep our minds open.

That means trying to understand other opinions, even if you don't agree with them. It also means trying new ways of doing things. It can spark exciting new ideas of your own.

School offers plenty of opportunities to open your mind: in class, through new activities and by making new friends. To help you approach new experiences, ask yourself questions:

• If you're nervous about trying something, ask: What's stopping me?

• If someone says something you disagree with, ask: Why might they have that opinion?

Let your ideas flow

Mind-mapping is a great way to see how your ideas connect and it's simple to do.

1. Draw a circle in the middle of a page. Inside, write the big idea that you'd like to explore – perhaps a problem, a task or a goal.

2. Using different colours, draw branches from the circle like legs on a spider, and label it with something that might help you explore the idea.

3. Draw more branches from these ideas in the same way.

4. Keep going until you've filled the page. See how your ideas have spread?

Celebrate your small wins

By celebrating, you make your achievements more memorable. They can help you to look forward to succeeding when you face a similar challenge.

Why not plan a small reward for yourself for next time you master a new skill or finish a task? It could be something as small as listening to your favourite song or making your favourite snack.

THE FOUNDATIONS OF FRIENDSHIP

Seeing your friends is often the best part of school life. Just seeing people every day won't always keep friendships strong, though – we need to **nurture** them.

Try active listening

Listening carefully to what someone else is saying so that you understand them better is an important part of being **compassionate**. This is called "active listening".

It means tuning into the other person and giving them all your attention while they're talking. This will help you to get inside someone else's head so that you can understand their emotions.

Learn more

Don't assume that if you've known someone for a long time, you know everything about them. Invite a friend to share things that are important to them. Perhaps their family has interesting traditions or there's a story or song very close to their heart.

You could organise something as simple as having lunch together, each bringing your favourite home-cooked dish. Perhaps you could have a film night when you show each other films that you each enjoy. Be sure to ask *why* these things mean a lot.

Help friends in need

We all need help sometimes, and it's important that we're there for our friends when they need us.

Here are some helpful tips for supporting a friend:

- Listen carefully and let them speak without interrupting.
- Show that you're listening by nodding and looking at them as they speak.
- Let your friend know that their feelings matter and that it's ok to feel the way they do.
- Ask what they would like from you, such as help finding further support.
- Check in on your friend after the conversation and make sure they're ok.

FAMILY TIME

It's easy to settle into a routine at home, but it's worth setting time aside to talk and laugh together.

Mix up your daily routine

Scientists have discovered that mixing up a daily routine boosts your brain and makes you happier. Unplanned adventures, even in your own neighbourhood, can bring you closer to others and help you to discover new places too.

This also helps to make long-lasting memories, which can help families to stay close.

You could trying practising mindfulness during your family adventures. Soak up the details, sounds and scents rather than rushing through the experience.

Make small changes

Just small things can make a difference to family time. You could try out a "no screens at the dinner table" rule, and focus on talking about each other's days.

Celebrating family traditions

Celebrating family traditions is another good way to strengthen bonds.

A tradition is a **custom** or belief that's passed down through families and cultures. The word comes from the Latin for "deliver" or "hand over".

Your family may have special traditions already, large or small. You may simply enjoy cooking together or curling up together to watch a favourite TV show. There's always a chance to make new traditions, too. This could be as simple as choosing a particular time for a catch-up or a walk at weekends.

If you'd like to plan something bigger, you could follow these tips.

• Trying something different.

• Think about the traditions your family already has and what kind of things you know you enjoy.

• Ask older adults in your family for ideas. They may remember traditions they had as children, which they may enjoy reviving.

• Brainstorm new ideas, jotting lots down before thinking about your favourites.

• Keep a **memento**. You could display a photo or souvenir to remind your family all year long of the fun that you had.

TAKING ME TIME

The evening can be the best time to take time for yourself. You might have a hobby that you enjoy. It's also important just to let your thoughts roam free by daydreaming.

What is daydreaming?

Daydreaming is letting your mind wander around ideas, thoughts and experiences that aren't happening right now, like memories or plans for the future.

Research shows that we spend nearly half of our day daydreaming, so it's good to practise doing it in a positive way.

How daydreaming is good for you

Disappearing into a daydream lets your mind escape when things are difficult. It also helps you to deal with worries and fears. For example, imagining how you're going to speak up in class is like practising the scenario in your head, which can make you feel calmer and in control.

Psychologist and author Erin Westgate thinks that we should all make time to daydream. "Thinking for pleasure can be a powerful tool to shape our emotions," she said.

Mindful moments

If your mind is unable to stop replaying difficult thoughts, try practising mindfulness. Listen to the sounds around you or focus on your breathing. Then you can guide your daydreams back in a positive direction.

Daydreaming also boosts creativity and lets you explore limitless new worlds.

Ready, set – daydream

Find a time when your attention isn't needed. Start by focusing on a happy memory or imagining a future success, like scoring a goal in the World Cup. You could also include favourite people in your daydreams.

To spark creativity, think about interesting ideas – and see where your mind takes you.

CHOOSE TO SNOOZE zzzzzz

It can be a challenge keeping to good sleep habits. These tips will help you to feel rested and ready for anything that the next day throws at you.

Stick to a bedtime

Going to bed at about the same time every night helps your body to get used to a schedule and fall asleep more easily. Choose a good bedtime by thinking about how much sleep you'd like to get (eight hours is about right) and when you have to get up.

Wind down before bed

Try to spend about an hour before bed relaxing so that your body and mind are ready for sleep. To use this time wisely, break it up into three 20-minute parts.

- **20 minutes:** To ease your mind, get your school bag, clothes and lunch ready for tomorrow.

- **20 minutes:** Take time to shower, brush your teeth and change into your pyjamas.

- **20 minutes:** Do something relaxing, like reading a book, listening to calming music or meditating.

Don't sabotage your sleep

What you eat and do during the day can affect your sleep too.

- Try to avoid drinks and food that contain caffeine (like fizzy drinks, tea and chocolate) after lunchtime.

- Exercise can help you to feel more tired, but not within a couple of hours of your bedtime.

- Try not to use devices for at least two hours before bed. The light from the screens – even small screens – can trick your body into thinking that it's daytime.

Stay steady

It's tempting to sleep in at the weekend, but oversleeping on some days can interfere with your sleep rhythms for the rest of the week. Wake up at your usual time or as close to it as you can, to stay well rested all week.

CREATING A SELF-CARE KIT

If you feel sad, having a self-care kit can come in handy. This type of kit is a collection of items that bring you comfort and help you to relax.

Think about what to include

The most important thing about a self-care kit is that it contains items that are helpful to you. They'll be different from anyone else's.

You could include photos of the people and animals you love; a special treasure, toy or book; something that smells or feels nice, such as a squishy ball; or cards or notes from friends and family.

You might keep them in a soft pouch, a plastic container or a small box.

Enjoy your kit

Whenever you're not feeling good, you can turn to your self-care kit and choose something to help you feel better. Over time, you might swap items in and out of your kit, depending on what feels most useful.

Talk about your kit

One of the best ways we can take care of our wellbeing is to talk about our feelings.

You may want to show a parent, sibling or a friend your self-care kit. You can talk about what it is and explain how the items help to support you when you need it.

Who knows? You may inspire them to make a self-care kit for themselves, and then you can give them some tips on getting started.

STRANGE BUT TRUE

DID YOU KNOW?

Mars is called the Red Planet because of its red colouring. This red colour is caused by large amounts of iron oxide – otherwise known as rust – which covers the surface of the planet.

DAYS OUT FOR DUST BUSTERS

Strange stories are forever scattered across everyday news. Some can make us smile by simply telling us about people having fun.

Having a "wheelie" good day out

When Kris Nesbitt was asked by a friend to take out their bin, he took it to the extreme. Instead of leaving it for rubbish collectors, he took it to the park.

They swung on the swings, slid down the slide and relaxed on a bench. The bin tired Nesbitt out, though. The bin was "difficult to fling around", he said.

Happy Henry's vacuum vacation

It's not easy being Henry Hoover: he spends his life being dragged along carpets, pushed under sofas and poked into dusty corners.

One owner decided to give his vacuum cleaner a well-earned break. Henry was taken on walks in the park, pushed on the swings and even treated to his own fish-and-chip supper.

CURIOUS COSTUMES

Sometimes odd news stories can originate from attention-grabbing publicity stunts.

Inflatable tactics to scare seagulls

Blackpool Zoo is expanding its team to include someone willing to dress up in an inflatable costume to imitate a bird. It is hoped they will be able to stop seagulls from stealing food from visitors and animals.

The zoo has tried using kites and plastic owls, but seagulls are very intelligent and quickly learn that those plastic pretenders don't present a real threat.

The employers described the ideal candidate as "friendly, energetic and outgoing".

Real OR rubbish?

Bear or not?

A video posted online showed a small sun bear in Hangzhou Zoo, China, standing on its back legs. The poster commented that this made the creature look suspiciously like a person wearing a bear suit.

A zoo official denied the charge, saying that the extremely high temperatures meant that anyone in a furry costume "would not last more than a few minutes before collapsing".

Is this story real or have we told a bear-faced lie?*

***Real!** The zoo publicly denied the charge, writing a social media post from the point of view of a sun bear named Angela.

Curious cat costume causes a stir

American actor Jared Leto dressed up as a giant blue-cream Birman cat to go to the Met Gala, a big fundraising party in New York.

Leto was inspired by a cat called Choupette, who belonged to a famous fashion designer called Karl Lagerfeld. Lagerfeld, who died in 2019, was the theme of the party.

The real Choupette stayed at home in Paris, where she has two maids and an iPad® of her own.

SEEKING A PRIDE
In Ireland, 252 people put on big-cat costumes to try to set a record for the largest gathering of people dressed as lions.

MISTAKEN FOR ALIENS

Is the truth about life in space really out there? Some people thought they'd found it on Earth.

Spooked by a flying saucer

When Dr James Danoff-Burg was giving a tour to a group of tourists in Florida, US, he spotted this unusual shape in the sky. The group watched as the spaceship shape appeared overhead.

Danoff-Burg posted pictures of the **UFO** online and they were soon shared, sparking fears that it was evidence of an alien invasion.

It was, in fact, a special type of cloud called a "lenticular cloud", which can look like a spaceship (or a stack of pancakes).

Would you have been fooled?

Dog walker's beach discovery

While Dave McGirr was walking his dog along Criccieth Beach in Wales, he spotted a strange-looking creature. It was six metres long, with brown tentacles and shiny white scales.

McGirr was determined to find out what it was. He took a photo and posted it online in the hope that someone might be able to help identify the "alien-like" creature. His search was successful: it was actually a six-metre piece of driftwood covered in gooseneck barnacles.

Gooseneck barnacles live on hard surfaces, such as rocks.

The existence of aliens has not yet been proven ...

Fisherman finds alien dragon

Angler Roman Fedortsov was used to finding relatively strange sea creatures on his fishing trips.

He was stunned, however, to land a particularly alien-like "baby dragon". The pale pink creature had large eyes, a long tail and what looked like wings sticking out from its sides. The image quickly racked up thousands of likes on Instagram.

It has since been identified as a chimaera, though — a kind of fish also known as a ghost shark.

COLOSSAL COLLECTIONS

The collector puzzled by his loft

When Florian Kastenmeier was clearing out his attic, he discovered a colourful little puzzle – a Rubik's Cube. The toy puzzles were a big craze 40 years ago, and 450 million of the colourful cubes have been sold since.

Florian became a fan and his passion for collecting the puzzles began. By 2022, he owned 1,519, and had been awarded the **Guinness World Record** for the largest collection of rotating puzzles in the world.

Florian has just one final puzzle to solve: where can he keep them all?

A deliciously rare collection

Nick Franklin has been a fan of *Charlie and the Chocolate Factory* ever since he was a child. He now has a collection of Willy Wonka-themed items, such as a Wonka chocolate bar, a golden ticket and a life-sized model of Augustus Gloop.

Franklin the super fan stores his collectibles in a special room in his house, which he has nicknamed the "Wonka wing". He's hoping to achieve a world record for his fabulous collection of Willy Wonka objects.

Gnome ... but not alone

A couple in South Molton, UK, had some unexpected arrivals in their garden: gnomes.

Christine and Stephen Lock were puzzled when the little statues started arriving at their home. Seven came along in quick **succession**, including one that was sent by post from France.

No one explained why the gnomes kept appearing, and whoever was responsible for sending the gnomes remained a mystery. In any case, the couple love their cheery statues and have even bought a little house for them.

A record-setting mooseum

Ruth Klossner has moo-re of an interest in cows than most people do. The Minnesota woman has loved the animals for decades, and in 2022 held a Guinness World Records title for collecting the most cow-related objects.

Her home is referred to as the Cow Collector's Mooseum because she displays all 19,827 items, including cow-themed toys, snow globes and figurines.

"If it's **bovine**, it's fine," she said.

Klossner estimates that the collection is now more valuable than her house.

Muggle mum's magical collection

A Harry Potter fan has created her own wizarding world with collectibles that are worth about £82,000. Carla Rodriguez of Maryland, US, has spent years collecting books, clocks, clothes, figures, jewellery, toys, wands and a rug.

She fell in love with author J.K. Rowling's fantasy world while decorating her young son's bedroom in 2016. Since then, her collection has grown to 1,000 items – including a necklace worth more than £5,700 – and now fills one whole room in her house.

A very impressive collection

Brian Trauman, from New Jersey, US, is officially the owner of the world's most extensive collection of sweets dispensers. He has 5,548 Pez dispensers to his name.

"I started the quest to 'get them all' in 1999," Trauman said, referring to a past Pez advertising slogan. "I didn't know how many that might be."

He says that some of his dispensers are worth more than £8,000. Others, however, have a more personal value – such as a Pez Yoda, the all-knowing character in *Star Wars*, which his sister gave him when he was studying law.

HOW MUCH?

Were these eye-popping prices worth paying, do you think? Some people thought so ...

Shock over far-fetched fruit price

A single jackfruit was once spotted on sale in Borough Market, London, for an eye-watering £160. When a photo was shared thousands of times on social media, many people in Brazil – where jackfruit can cost less than £1 – were stunned by the price.

The reason why the fruit was so expensive is that it does not grow in cold climates, so it is difficult to find it fresh in the UK.

Toy fan makes a huge profit

A *Star Wars* toy that was bought for 99p at a supermarket in 1983 has sold for £2,000 at an auction. The action figure was still in its original packaging and was part of a 37-toy collection that was being sold by a *Star Wars* superfan. The collection reached a total value of £37,500.

David Wilson Turner, from Hansons Auctioneers who organised the sale, said, "The *Star Wars* phenomenon is a force to be reckoned with."

Surreal spending

A **surrealist** artist called Salvador Dalí designed this lobster phone in 1936. There are three of these creations on display in the UK. In 2018, one was bought for £853,000.

The richest flavour of ice cream

Here's the scoop: the most expensive ice cream in the world is now selling for over £5,700 a serving.

The Japanese ice cream company Cellato calls its new flavour *byakuya*, meaning "white night" in Japanese. The Italian-style gelato, which uses ingredients imported from Italy, is made with two types of cheese, white truffles and edible gold leaf.

A Cellato representative said that it took the company more than a year to develop the fancy flavour, "with a lot of trial and error to get the taste right".

WOODEN WONDERS

University opens wooden building

The wooden building.

Nanyang Technological University in Singapore has unveiled a new building made almost entirely from wood. Named after the ancient Greek goddess of Earth, Gaia, it's designed to make visitors feel as if they're walking through trees.

Toyo Ito, who designed it, told a US news network that he wanted to create a "connection with – and a feeling of – nature".

Wheeling out a wooden car

It's only ever had one owner, it has six wheels and it's never going to rust – although it might attract some strange looks.

A Hustler **kit car** made in the 1980s by John Brazier from Bristol, UK, sold for £2,500 at auction. Fewer than 400 Hustlers were built, and most were made from **fibreglass** rather than wood.

"I'd love to see it occasionally being driven around," Brazier told *The Guardian* newspaper.

Wood city planned in Sweden

An ambitious plan to build a "wood city" in Stockholm, Sweden, has been revealed. It is believed that the work will be the world's largest wood construction project. It will contain 2,000 homes, 7,000 offices, cafés, restaurants and shops.

It's hoped that the wooden buildings will help the environment. As they grow, trees absorb carbon dioxide from the air and store the carbon. However, wood needs to be gathered from forests where new trees are planted to replace old ones and not be the cause of **deforestation**.

Annica Anas, who works for the company organising the project, said that it was important for them to "make a positive difference".

Stockholm is already home to many wooden buildings.

RIDICULOUS WRONGDOING

These cases have all been cracked – but they all sound crackers! Can you tell which are real and which are criminally misleading?

Thieves start off on the wrong foot

Some shoe-snatchers in the city of Huancayo, Peru, might have thought they'd hit the jackpot after they ran off with more than 200 stolen trainers from a shoe shop.

However, although it was a huge haul of shoes, every one of them was for the right foot – there was not a pair among them.

Did the thieves really have nothing "left" – or are we pulling your (right) leg?

***Real!** The shop owner said that although *pairs* of the shoes would have a value of more than £10,000, the thieves might have some trouble selling them.

No loo roll for coronation

All the details of the planning for Queen Elizabeth II's coronation are kept in an **archive**. Historians looking back found a real tissue issue.

Buckingham Palace staff woke up on the morning of the celebration to discover that much of the loo paper had gone missing. They had to work quickly to solve the problem, so that no one would be caught short.

Is this story real or have we flushed out a fib?

***Real!** The historians studying the documents believe that someone spied a chance for free toilet paper and raided the palace stores.

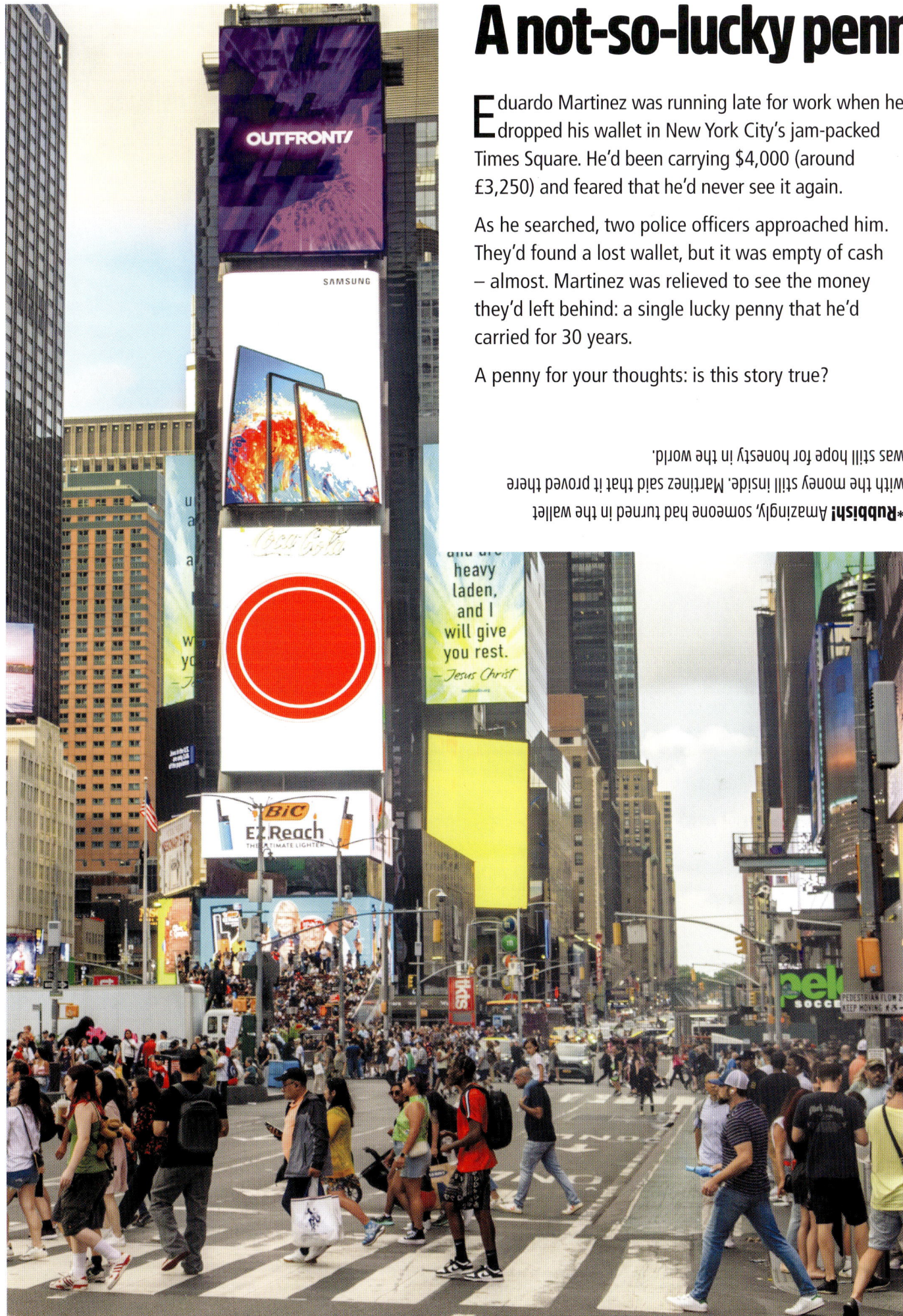

A not-so-lucky penny

Eduardo Martinez was running late for work when he dropped his wallet in New York City's jam-packed Times Square. He'd been carrying $4,000 (around £3,250) and feared that he'd never see it again.

As he searched, two police officers approached him. They'd found a lost wallet, but it was empty of cash – almost. Martinez was relieved to see the money they'd left behind: a single lucky penny that he'd carried for 30 years.

A penny for your thoughts: is this story true?

*Rubbish! Amazingly, someone had turned in the wallet with the money still inside. Martinez said that it proved there was still hope for honesty in the world.

GLOSSARY

addictive difficult to stop doing even when it's bad for you

AI artificial intelligence; a computer system that learns from experience and does jobs that would usually need human intelligence

analyse study information closely in order to learn about something

angler person who catches fish using a hook tied to a fishing line

anonymous an unknown identity; something without a name

archaeologists experts who study history through ancient objects

archive collection of historical records

artefacts human-made objects of historical interest

aspects features of an object

asteroid rocky object moving around the Sun

auction sale process where the person willing to pay the most wins

Baltic related to a region surrounding the Baltic Sea, mainly in Northern Europe

BCE Before the Common Era; before the year zero

bog soft, wet, muddy ground

bovine related to cows

carbon dioxide gas that traps the Sun's heat in a layer around Earth, making temperatures rise

CE Common Era; after the year zero

collaborative involving two or more people or groups working together

compassionate kind and caring towards someone else

conservationists people who work to protect the environment and wildlife

constrain restrict the scope or movement of something or someone

controversial causing disagreement

cost-of-living crisis situation in which the cost of food and household bills is increasing more quickly than the amount people get paid

creatives people who do artistic work for a living

critical urgent and important

cross-breeding producing offspring with parents of two different breeds

cues signals for someone to do or say something

culprit person responsible for a crime or other misbehaviour

culture behaviours and ideas linking societies or communities

custom behaviour linked to a particular place, time period or group of people

customs officials people whose job is to check that travellers aren't taking goods into a country illegally

cygnets baby swans

daunting difficult or frightening

deforestation the process of trees being cleared on a large scale, often for farming

displaced moved from its usual position by something or someone else

DNA chemical carrying information about a species

domain particular area

domestic living in a home alongside humans

domesticated trained and bred so that they can live in a home alongside humans

donor person who gives something for free to another person or cause

droughts long periods of little or no rain that cause water shortages

emerged came out and became visible

emissions waste products created when burning fuel

empathy ability to understand and share someone else's feelings

enclosure living space surrounded by barriers

endangered at risk of dying out

entities things that have their own identities

ethics rules or expectations that define good and bad behaviour

evolved gradually changed along the family tree, from parents to children, over an extremely long period of time

exhibition group of related displays

exhibits objects that are on display

exoskeletons hard protective skins that hold creatures' shapes without bones

fast refrain from eating some or all kinds of food, particularly for religious reasons

fibreglass a light, strong material made from plastic and glass fibres

FIFA international football (soccer) association

filament bulbs light bulbs that create light by heating a wire

fjord a long, deep, narrow body of seawater that reaches far inland

fossil fuels fuels, like coal and crude oil, that are made from decayed prehistoric plants and animals and are dug from the ground

genre style or category (of books, films, music or art)

gills organ used by fish and other water creatures to breathe

greengrocer's shop that sells fruit and vegetables

Guinness World Record one of a collection of records of people's achievements, which were originally released annually in a book

hibernation the act of reducing activity to use less energy, similar to very deep sleeping, which is how many creatures survive the winter

humanoid robot that looks and acts like a human

icebreaker ship designed to break ice as it moves through the sea

indigenous people people who originally lived in a place before others came and took over

innovative using new approaches to solve a problem or achieve a goal

inspiration experience that encourages you to do or think something

inspired created or affected by a different experience

intimidating threatening or frightening

kit car car that is bought as separate parts and must be put together

landfill rubbish that is buried instead of being reused or recycled

larvae young forms of insects that usually look different from the adults

LED bulbs light bulbs that create light from electronic circuits

ligament part of a body that connects bones to other bones

literacy ability to read and write

livelihood how someone earns money to survive and thrive

local authorities organisations that are officially responsible for public services and facilities in a particular area

manhole covers heavy lids that hide the entrances to tunnels leading down to drains or underground railways

manipulate control things physically and skilfully

memento object kept as a reminder of something else

mimic copy the behaviour of someone or something else

mollusc part of a scientific grouping of species that includes squids, snails and shellfish

monarch king or queen

mosaics artworks made from small pieces of stone glued into a pattern

movement group of people trying to make big changes because of a particular idea

myths stories shared between people over many years, which may or may not be true

NASA US government agency responsible for space research and exploration

native originally living in the area

nonnas grandmothers in Italian

nurture look after something while it grows

outline plan that organises the main events in a story

palaeontologist expert who studies fossils

paralysis condition in which you can't move your muscles

parasites living things that live on another species

performance artist someone who performs art using their own body, often requiring high levels of skill or fitness

petrified extremely scared; frozen in fear

platinum jubilee celebration of a 70th anniversary

pollinators creatures that spread pollen between plants

prank practical joke

predators creatures that catch and eat other creatures

prehistory time before humans made records of events

prey creatures that are caught and eaten by other creatures

psychologists experts who study how people think

pun joke making use of words with multiple meanings or words that sound alike

quilt large piece of fabric made from different pieces of fabric sewn together

quirky odd, often in a fun way

realism representation that is true to life

rebels people refusing to follow the rules of their leaders

remote far away from other places

renegade individual who ignores rules about behaviour

replica copy of an object, often smaller

retrieve collect; get back

root vegetables plants' roots that we can eat, like carrots and potatoes

salt pans very flat and featureless areas formed when seawater dries up

scheme set of rules or guidelines

self-esteem how you feel about yourself

sewage waste from lots of people

shards pieces of an object that has shattered

shredding controlled surfing that creates dramatic spray

skin cancer condition in which skin cells grow out of control, which can be caused by too much sun

skip big metal waste container, often seen on building sites

skydiver someone who jumps out of planes with a parachute

slackens dips down and feels loose

smuggled moved secretly and illegally

social related to relationships or interactions

specimen example of something kept as a record for research

spontaneous doing things naturally or on impulse, without planning

stollen traditional German cake, a bit like a sweet bread, made with fruit and nuts and dusted with icing sugar

stratosphere layer of the atmosphere from about 10 to 50 kilometres above Earth's surface

succession sequence; one after another

supercapacitor device for storing large amounts of electric charge, which can be released quickly for power

superstition belief or behaviour based on faith in luck or magic

surrealist related to showing unusual ideas, thoughts and dreams rather than life-like everyday things

taut pulled tight

televised shown on television

tentacles flexible and movable body parts used for holding things, moving and feeding

thrives grows and succeeds

UFO unidentified flying object; something reported flying through the sky that cannot be explained (often thought to be an alien flying saucer)

ultrasound sound that is higher pitched than humans can hear

Vikings community of people from Scandinavia who invaded and settled in nearby places across northern Europe around 1,000 years ago

vocalisations sounds used to communicate and express feelings

waterline line marking the level of the surface of the water

wheel large, flat cylinder (of cheese)

x-ray picture taken of the skeleton using light that our eyes cannot detect

zest outer layer of the peel of citrus fruits

zip wire long wire along which people can slide from one place to another

INDEX

A
acrobatics 89, 187
aeroplanes (planes) 88-89, 165
air guitar 174
aliens 220-221
Amazon rainforest 62-63, 67, 71, 94
amphibians 42-45
Amur tigers 35
Antarctic 69, 93, 171
Antarctica 70, 93, 169
ants 58-59
arachnophobia 60
archaeology 96-99
architecture 228-229
art
    animal artists 10-11, 49
    artificial intelligence (AI) 104-105
    cave paintings 131
    food art 132-135, 140-141, 157
    modern art 144-145
    museums 145-149
    mysteries 142-143
    street art 136, 138-139
    unusual places 136-137
artificial intelligence (AI) 36, 102-105
asteroids 114
astronauts 112, 115
audiobooks 123

B
badgers 21
bats 34
beaches 68, 175, 221
bears 20, 71, 218
Beatles 104
birds 11, 15, 18-19, 21, 22-23, 31, 46-49, 74, 84, 170, 218
board games 196
books 116-125
breakfast 34, 201
British Museum 99, 147
bumblebee bat 34
bumblebees 56
Burmese pythons 41

C
camouflage 46
cats 28-29, 35, 167, 219
caves 92, 96, 99, 130, 164
centipedes 61
cheese 153-155, 159, 171, 174, 227
chimaera 221
climate change 65, 68, 71, 83, 102
clothing 76, 85
cockatoo 11, 14
collections 222-225
communication in animals 36, 48
coral reefs 65
costumes 184, 218-219
Covid-19 pandemic 121
crafting 84-85, 134, 140-141, 157
crocodiles 38
cross-breeding 51
cycling 78-79

D
daydreaming 208-209
dinosaurs 96-97, 184
dogs 10, 24-27, 35, 42, 71, 98, 111
dolphins 15
dormice 75
dreams 54
droughts 68, 71
ducks 21

E
Earth Day 83
ebikes 79
electricity 80-81
elephants 8, 14
emissions 78
emotions
    animals 12-14
    humans 200
empathy 12
emus 23, 47
energy saving 80-81
environment 62-73, 78-79
exoskeletons 57

F
fake cake 140-141
family 206-207
feelings 12-15, 200-201
festivals 90, 138-139, 174-175, 183
fish 50-51, 157, 221
floods 69
flying frogs 44
food
    as art 132-133, 157
    delivery 188
    fight 183
    flavours 158-159

lab-grown meat 108-109
nacho recipe 154-155
restaurants 178-179
salad recipe 160-161
super-sized 152-153
vegetables 85, 156-157
football 190-191
fossil fuels 68, 78
foxes 35
friendship
   animals 14-15
   humans 204-205
frogs 15, 43-45

G

games 171, 196
gastropods 61
gecko lizard 33
gibbons 34
gnomes 223
goldfish 51
great crested newts 42
grey squirrels 35
gulls 19, 218

H

habitats 74-75
hamsters 113
hawks 47
heatwaves 72-73
hibernation 42
hobby horses 184
homes 172-173
horses 13, 184
hot air balloons 164
hula-hooping 186

I

icebergs 70
ice hockey 181, 189
ice levels 69
indigenous people 67
insects 56-59, 66, 137

J

jackdaw 22
jellyfish 55
jewellery 77, 99, 224
jobs 168-171

K

kakapo 49
kites 175-177
Komodo dragon 32-33

L

lab-grown meat 108-109
larvae 57
laughter 16-17
lemons 153
libraries 118-121
listening 204
lizards 32-33, 39, 67
Louvre 147

M

magpies 18-19
Mars 215
meat 108-109
meerkats 12
Met Gala 219

Metropolitan Museum
of Art 147
mice 15, 75, 112
Milky Way 100
mindfulness 206, 208
mind-mapping 203
Minions 142
monster myths 37
moths 57
mountain art 137
museums 99, 127, 137, 145-149
music 10, 89, 104, 157
myna birds 74
myths 37

N

nacho recipe 154-155
NASA 112-114
national parks 29, 43, 67, 164
newts 42
Niue 65

O

oceans 46, 50-55, 65, 69-70
octopuses 54
otter 22

P

panda 30
parasites 36, 52
parrots 48-49
peacock 31
penguins 46, 71, 169
phones 106-107
pickleball 187
pigs 11

237

pine martens 35
pipistrelle bat 34
pizza 153, 159
planes (aeroplanes) 88-89, 165
plastics 77, 82
platinum jubilee 134
polar bears 71
polio 110
pollinators 57
Pompeii 98
poo 110-111
predators 19, 44, 46, 52, 74

R

rainbow sea slug 55
rainforests 62-63, 67, 71, 94
rats 16-17
reading 116-125
recycling 77, 84-85
red squirrels 35
reptiles 31-33, 38-41
rescues 92-95
restaurants 178-179
robots 102-105
rock climbing 193
rollercoasters 168
roller skating 194
rubbish 76-77, 84-85
Rubik's Cube 222

S

salad recipe 160-161
salt pans 58
school 106-107, 202-203
seagulls 19, 218
seahorses 74
sealife 36-37, 50-55, 65-66, 221
sea turtles 66
seaweed 36

self-care kit 212-213
sewage 110
sharks 52-53
sheep 167
skydiving 86-90
Skywalker gibbons 34
sleep 164, 210-211
slugs 55, 61
smartphones 106-107
smiling 198
snails 61
snakes 31, 40-41
snorkelling 183
space 100, 112-115, 178, 214-215, 220
spiders 60
sport 180-195
squirrels 35
stratosphere 113
street art 136, 138-139
stunts 88-91
supercapacitor 79
sushi 153
Sutton Hoo 99
swans 170

T

teamwork 15, 197
tegu lizard 39
tentacles 54
theme parks 168
Thunberg, Greta 65
tigers 35
tightrope walking 89, 91
toads 42-43
tortoises 31, 39,
tourism 52, 107, 166-167
toys 77, 184, 222, 224, 226
trees 64, 83

trumpetfish 50
turtles 66

U

ultrasound waves 112

V

vacations 164-165
vegetables 85, 156-157
Vikings 37
vocalisations 16

W

walking 195
wasps 57
waste 76-77, 84-85, 110-111
water 50-55, 65, 71, 82, 135, 183
weather
   climate change 65, 68, 71, 83, 102
   droughts 68, 71
   floods 69
   heatwaves 72-73
wellbeing 195, 198-213
whales 36-37
Whanganui River 66
woodlands 75
wrestling 182
writing 126-129

Z

zip wire 89
zoos 12, 14, 30-31, 49, 74, 218

MORE BRILLIANT BOOKS FROM

COMING JULY 2025

Find out everything you need to know about the world of politics and the environment. These handy guides are packed with essential information and fascinating facts, with easy-to-understand explanations and ideas of ways you can make a difference.

The Week Junior Guide to Politics | 9781801995306 | Paperback | £7.99   The Week Junior Guide to the Environment | 9781801995856 | Paperback | £7.99

IMAGE CREDITS

Front cover: (mr) Sascha Burkard/Shutterstock; (tr) Germanskydiver/Shutterstock; (br) sruilk/Shutterstock; (mr) Simia Attentive/Shutterstock; (bl) Andrey Suslov/Shutterstock; (tl) Kuznetsov Alexey/Shutterstock; (m) Mega Pixel/Shutterstock; p3 Cornel Pop/Shutterstock; p4 (t) nasidastudio/Shutterstock; (b) object-photo/Shutterstock; p5 (tl) Mark Higgins/Shutterstock; (tr) ezpic/Shutterstock; (mr) HomeArt/Shutterstock; (b) Andrea Izzotti/Shutterstock; p6 (tl) nobeastsofierce/Shutterstock; (tr) New Africa/Shutterstock; (br) Kishimoto Takehiro @ gakugakugakugakugaku1; (bl) vipman/Shutterstock; p7 (tl) Engineer studio/Shutterstock; (tr) MyImages/Micha/Shutterstock; (ml) Roman Belogorodov/Shutterstock; (br) koya979/Shutterstock; pp8–9 Willyam Bradberry/Shutterstock; p10 (bg) Martial Red/Shutterstock; WarmWorld/Shutterstock p11 (t) Sutthiphong Chandaeng/Shutterstock; (b) Igor Stramyk/Shutterstock; Miras W/Shutterstock; Milano M/Shutterstock p12 (t) Rosa Jay/Shutterstock; (b) Mint Images on Offset/Shutterstock; p13 (m) Shawn Hamilton/Shutterstock; (l) ArtHeart/Shutterstock; pp14–15 (bg) nattanan726/Shutterstock; ArtHeart/Shutterstock p15 (t) Andrea Izzotti/Shutterstock; (m) Kseniia Vladimirovna/Shutterstock; (r) both Eric Isselee/Shutterstock; p16 (m) Ian Dyball/Shutterstock; ArtHeart/Shutterstock; p17 (t) Ezume Images/Shutterstock; (m) Jan Bray/Shutterstock; pp18-19 (bg) Chinch/Shutterstock; p18 (m) Rose Marinelli/Shutterstock; p19 (t) CCBY Naturalis/Alexander Schippers; (t) Brsznca/Shutterstock; (r) Mario Modesto Mata/Shutterstock; (r) pavla/Shutterstock; p20 (m) Eric Isselee/Shutterstock; (l) Moving Moment/Shutterstock; p21 (m) Ondrej Prosicky/Shutterstock; (r) Ondrej Chvatal/Shutterstock; p22 (l) Tanya_Terekhina/Shutterstock; (m) Only Fabrizio/Shutterstock; Saltus/Shutterstock; (bg) William Barton/Shutterstock; p23 (m) Shirley Jayne Photography/Shutterstock; (r) mark higgins/Shutterstock; (bg) Deephill Media/Shutterstock; pp24–25 alexei_tm/Shutterstock; p24 (l) alexei_tm/Shutterstock; Chinch/Shutterstock; pp26–27 alexei_tm/Shutterstock; p28 (t) art studio ideas/Shutterstock; (m) IrinaK/Shutterstock; (bg) Kay Cee Lens and Footages/Shutterstock; p29 (t) laschi/Shutterstock; (t) Net Vector/Shutterstock; (r) Creative Cat Studio/Shutterstock p30 (t) Svetsol/Shutterstock; (l) clarst5/Shutterstock; p31 (t) TraceyRI/Shutterstock; (m) Eric Isselee/Shutterstock; (r) Svetlana Foote/Shutterstock; pp32–33 (bg) miroslav chytil/Shutterstock; p34 (l) teekayu/Shutterstock; (r) Roziline/Shutterstock; p35 (t) Rudmer Zwerver/Shutterstock; (l) tgladkova/Shutterstock; (r) Eric Isselee/Shutterstock; pp36–37 Ahturner/Shutterstock; p36 Stramless/Shutterstock; p37 gameover / Alamy Stock Photo; p38 yishii/Shutterstock; p39 (t) Creative Stock Studio/Shutterstock; (bg) Elenamiv/Shutterstock; (m) DenisNata/Shutterstock; (l) Mirelle/Shutterstock; p40 (t) Kurit afshen/Shutterstock; (m) Wirestock Creators/Shutterstock; (l) Mohamad alias/Shutterstock; p41 (m) Heiko Kiera/Shutterstock; (lm) CBS via Getty Images; (l) Vector Tradition/Shutterstock; p42 (t) Peter_Fleming/Shutterstock; (m) Latent Image/Shutterstock; (l) Dirk Ercken/Shutterstock; p43 (bg) caseyjadew/Shutterstock; (t) Queensland Government – Department of Environment, Science and Innovation; (b) cynoclub/Shutterstock; p44 Dennis J Gaspersz/Shutterstock; p45 (t) petrdd/Shutterstock; (m) Kletr/Shutterstock; p46 (t) Illustration-store/Shutterstock; (bg) Andrei Armiagov/Shutterstock; (m) sonio_heeee/Shutterstock; p47 (t) Richard Seeley/Shutterstock; (bg) MikNik/Shutterstock; (r) Herman Vlad/Shutterstock; (rbg) Dalibor Sevaljevic/Shutterstock; (r) JoshingtonDC/Shutterstock; p48 funstarts33/Shutterstock; p49 (t) Bruyu/Shutterstock; (r) cynoclub/Shutterstock; (r) Hurst Photo/Shutterstock; (r) irin-k/Shutterstock p50 (bg) p50 (bg) Rich Carey/Shutterstock; (l) Rich Carey/Shutterstock; (m) Rich Carey/Shutterstock; (r) Johannes Kornelius/Shutterstock; p51 (t) malgosia janicka/Shutterstock; (bg) slowmotiongli/Shutterstock; (m) briddy/Shutterstock; pp52–53 (bg) Max Topchii/Shutterstock; p52 (l) wildestanimal/Shutterstock; p53 (r) frantisekhojdysz/Shutterstock; pp54–55 (bg) Solarisys/Shutterstock; p54 (m) Evikka/Shutterstock; p55 (t) Vicky Barlow / Alamy Stock Photo; (r) grafxart/Shutterstock; pp56–57 (bg) MN84/Shutterstock; p56 (t) irin-k/Shutterstock; (m) Vitalii Hulai/

Shutterstock; p57 (t) Karel Bock/Shutterstock; (r) Amani A/Shutterstock; pp58–59 (bg) frank60/Shutterstock; p58 (l) iStock.com/pic4you; (r) Pavel Krasensky/Shutterstock; p59 (r) parianto/Shutterstock; p60 (bg) CeltStudio/Shutterstock; (r) Lipatova Maryna/Shutterstock; p61 (t) Mike John Brown/Shutterstock; (m) skifbook/Shutterstock; (r) ajt/Shutterstock; pp62-63 (bg) PopTika/Shutterstock p62 (m) PopTika/Shutterstock; ArtHeart/Shutterstock; pp62–63 Panga Media/Shutterstock; p64 (t) HomeArt/Shutterstock; (b) Helissa Grundemann/Shutterstock; p65 (t) kkshxt/Shutterstock; (m) Liv Oeian/Shutterstock; (b) SCStock Pics/Shutterstock; (bg) Romolo Tavani/Shutterstock p66 (t) GoodStudio/Shutterstock; (m) Laverne Nash/Shutterstock; (bl) Alex Manders; (br) irin-k/ Shutterstock; p67 (t) Robert Wyatt / Alamy Stock Photo; (b) Maris Maskalans/Shutterstock; p68 (t) JosepPerianes/Shutterstock; (b) Dishev/Shutterstock; p69 (t) ABDULKHALEK SAAD/Shutterstock; (b) Trendspace/Shutterstock; p70 Michael Milner via Getty Images; p71 (t) Ondrej Prosicky/Shutterstock; (b) Michael Dantas / AFP via Getty Images; pp72–73 (bg) Alex Erwin/Shutterstock; p72 (t) Tomas Ragina/Shutterstock; (bl) Mybona/Shutterstock; (br) VCG / Visual China Group via Getty Images; p73 (l) Mariyana (M)/Shutterstock; (r) Yellowj/Shutterstock; p74 (m) TungCheung/Shutterstock; (b) ChameleonsEye/Shutterstock; p75 (bg) Kozma 94/Shutterstock; p76 (all) NYS/Shutterstock; (b) Ernest Rose/Shutterstock; (bg) GreenSkyStudio/Shutterstock; p77 (t) create jobs 51/Shutterstock; (m) Alfmaler/Shutterstock; (b) Abdurzaq Alshami / Al Jazeera; pp78–79 Monkey Business Images/Shutterstock; (bl) NadyGinzburg/Shutterstock; pp80–81 (bg) fokke baarssen/Shutterstock; p80 (t) photographyfirm/Shutterstock; (b) Roman Samborskyi/Shutterstock; p81 (t) zblaster/Shutterstock; (b) Pixel-Shot/Shutterstock; pp82–83 (bg) terimma/Shutterstock; p82 (t) myboys.me/Shutterstock; (m) Milan Ivosevic/Shutterstock; (b) Dmitry Naumov/Shutterstock; p83 (t) Evgeny Atamanenko/Shutterstock; (b) Irina Wilhauk/Shutterstock; p84 (t) Takamon/Shutterstock; (b) ezpic/Shutterstock; p85 (t) Gaus Alex/Shutterstock; (bg) VOLGAVOLGA/Shutterstock; (m) Elena Medoks/Shutterstock; (bl) SashkaB/Shutterstock; (br) Stanislav Samoylik/Shutterstock; pp86–87 Mauricio Graiki/Shutterstock; p88 Associated Press / Alamy Stock Photo; p89 (bg) white clouds, blue sky Adhivaswut/Shutterstock; (t) MAXPPP / Alamy Stock Photo; (b) Dorset Media Service / Alamy Stock Photo; p90 (bg) Mauricio Graiki/Shutterstock; (b) New Africa/Shutterstock; p91 Abaca Press / Alamy Stock Photo; p92 (t) Stefan Balaz/Shutterstock; (b) Anadolu / Anadolu via Getty Images; p93 Associated Press / Alamy Stock Photo; p94 (bg) achiaos/Shutterstock; (b) Juan Barreto / AFP via Getty Images; p95 (t) Associated Press / Alamy Stock Photo; (b) AFP via Getty Images; p96-97 (bg) LindaPerez/Shutterstock; p97 (t) Mark_Kostich/Shutterstock; (b) sruilk/Shutterstock; p98 (t) Curioso.Photography/Shutterstock; (b) Simone Crespiatico/Shutterstock; p99 (t) lightphoto/iStock; (b) Associated Press / Alamy Stock Photo; p100 mozzyb/Shutterstock; pp102– 103 (bg) PopTika/Shutterstock; p102 (t) Jomic/Shutterstock; p103 (b) Associated Press / Alamy Stock Photo; pp104–105 (bg) Jomic/Shutterstock; p104 (t) terra.incognita/Shutterstock; (b) Ralf Liebhold/Shutterstock; p105 (t) Universal History Archive / Universal Images Group via Getty Images; (b) VCG/ Visual China Group via Getty Images; p106 (t) Calypso Art/Shutterstock; (b) Ground Picture/Shutterstock; p107 (t) BearFotos/Shutterstock; (tr) Ground Picture/Shutterstock; (b) Javier Ruiz/Shutterstock; p108 MaraZe/Shutterstock; p109 (t) DottedYeti/Shutterstock; (b) Tatjana Baibakova/Shutterstock; pp110–111 (m) nobeastsofierce/Shutterstock; p110 (tl) Alfmaler/Shutterstock; (t) koya979/Shutterstock; p111 (tl – fly) Alfmaler/Shutterstock; (tl – dog) trexwakeup/Shutterstock; (tr) Anna Hoychuck/Shutterstock; (b) Shchus/Shutterstock; pp112–113 (bg) DM7/Shutterstock; p113 (t) Alex Milan/Shutterstock; p114–115 (bg) mapush/Shutterstock; p115 (b) NASA Photo / Alamy Stock Photo; pp116–117 Stella_E/Shutterstock; p118 (t) Roman Sigaev/Shutterstock; (b) Stefan Holm/Shutterstock; p119 (tl) Celig/Shutterstock; (tr) vipman/Shutterstock; (b) wavebreakmedia/Shutterstock; p120 (t) vipman/Shutterstock; (ml) Westend61 on Offset/Shutterstock; (mm) Ken Wolter/Shutterstock; (mr) Rawpixel.com/Shutterstock; (bl) Rawpixel.com/Shutterstock; (br) Mix and Match Studio/Shutterstock; p121 pook2524/Shutterstock; p122 Romolo Tavani/Shutterstock; p123 Pixel-Shot/Shutterstock; pp124–125 (m) Billion Photos/Shutterstock; Kumer Oksana/Shutterstock; p124 (b) Ann Gaysorn/Shutterstock; p125 (t) Africa Studio/Shutterstock; (b) anek.soowannaphoom/Shutterstock; p126 hanapon1002/Shutterstock; p127 (t) VaLiza/Shutterstock; (b) Mia Stendal/Shutterstock; p128 (bg) Pand P Studio/Shutterstock; (m) ADDICTIVE STOCK/Shutterstock; (bgbr) Bigmouse108/Shutterstock; p129 (t) Uber Images/Shutterstock; (b) Ground Picture/Shutterstock; p130–131 (bg) Fadil Aziz/Alcibbum Photograph/The Image Bank via Getty Images; p132 (bg) GVV Studio/Shutterstock; (m) Raj Valley/Alamy Stock Photo; (b) Cover-Images/IMAGO; p133 (t) PA Images/Alamy Stock Photo; (m) Josh Edelson/AFP via Getty Images; (b) Kim Bainbridge; p134 (bg) PA Images/Alamy Stock Photo; p135 (t) The Standard/Chris Carter; (r) evemilla/iStock; (b) Jim Dyson/Getty Images Entertainment via Getty Images; (bg) StacieStauffSmith Photos/Shutterstock; p136 (t) Woman from Baku/Shutterstock; (b) b-hide the scene/Shutterstock; p137 (t) YueStock/Shutterstock; (b) ANP/Alamy Stock Photo; p138 (bg) Armend Nimani/AFP via Getty Images; p139 (t) Eddie Keogh/ Getty Images Sport via Getty Images; (l) EQRoy/Shutterstock; (r) New Africa/Shutterstock and stockphoto-graf/Shutterstock; p140 (t) La Gorda/Shutterstock; (b) Future Publishing Limited; (bg) Ailisa/Shutterstock; p141 (t) ra3rn/Shutterstock; (b) Future Publishing Limited; (bg) Ailisa/Shutterstock; p142 (r) wasantistock/iStock; p143 (tr) Kent Wildlife Trust; (tl) Na_Studio/Shutterstock; (b) Eduard Goricev/Shutterstock; p144 (m) Elizabeth_0102/Shutterstock; (b) jnumber9/Shutterstock; p145 (t) Ascannio/Shutterstock; (b) Hunter Bliss Images/Shutterstock; p146 (t) Stoniko/Shutterstock; (b) Pack-Shot/Shutterstock; p147 (t) Richie Chan/Shutterstock; (m) Wirestock Creators/Shutterstock; (b) Sean Pavone/Shutterstock; pp148-149 (bg) SeventyFour/Shutterstock; pp150-151 (bg) Zivica Kerkez/Shutterstock; p152 (bl) Ground Picture; (br) Guiness World Records; p153 (tl) Aflo Co. Ltd./Alamy Stock Photo; (tr) Nicholas Piccillo/Shutterstock; (m) Joshua Sterns/ Moment Open via Getty Images; (b) Ian 2010/Shutterstock; pp154-155 (bg) Brent Hofacker/Shutterstock; (t) Yeti studio/Shutterstock; p156 (bg) angiolina/Shutterstock; (m) photobeps/Shutterstock; (b) stas11/Shutterstock; p157 (t) Associated Press / Alamy Stock Photo; (m) LukaKikina/Shutterstock; (b) Kishimoto Takehiro @gakugakugakugakugaku1; p158 (m) DenisMArt/Shutterstock; (b) MERCURY studio/Shutterstock; p159 (bg) Nathaniel Noir / Alamy Stock Photo; pp160-161 (bg) nelea33/Shutterstock; pp162–163 (bg) Sergey-73/Shutterstock; p164 (t) Vitezslav Valka/Shutterstock; (b) Go Below Underground Adventures; p165 (t) BUI LE MANH HUNG/Shutterstock; (r) Airbnb x Shrek's Swamp, Alix McIntosh, 2023; p166 (bg) Lakechipotleorg; (l) Ground Picture/Shutterstock; p167 (b) Bob Pool/Shutterstock; Feifei Cui Paoluzzo via Getty Images; p168 (bg) iStock.com/Haxortech; p169 (t) New Africa/Shutterstock; (m) Ronsmith/Shutterstock; (r) fieldwork/Shutterstock; p170 (tl) Peter Dazeley via Getty Images; (bg) Thipwan/Shutterstock; p171 (tbg) onajourney/Shutterstock; (tl) Fertas/Shutterstock; (r) Lapina/Shutterstock; p172 (l) PA Images / Alamy Stock Photo; p173 (tbg) Mr Twister/Shutterstock; (mr) Stephen Rees/Shutterstock; (mr) doomu/Shutterstock; (l) Ruth Black/Shutterstock; p174 (t) Iana Alter/Shutterstock; (l) ComposedPix/Shutterstock; (r) AFP via Getty Images; p175 (t) Ian Reay/Shutterstock; (r) Robert Kneschke/Shutterstock; (r) leszczem/Shutterstock; pp176–177 (bg) Sergey Novikov/Shutterstock; p178 (bg) Alican Akcol/Shutterstock; (l) Dean Drobot/Shutterstock; (r) Engineer studio/Shutterstock; p179 (t) NTB / Alamy Stock Photo; (m) dpa picture alliance / Alamy Stock Photo; (r) Sergei Gapon via Getty Images; pp180–181 (bg) Oleksandr Osipov/Shutterstock; p182 (t) Vasyl Shulga/Shutterstock; ViDI Studio/Shutterstock; (m) AFP Contributor via Getty Images; p183 (tr) BearFotos/Shutterstock; (m) pics five/Shutterstock; (l) Richard Heathcote via Getty Images; p184 (l) marinat197/Shutterstock; (r) Roman Belogorodov/Shutterstock; p185 (r) Chung Sung-Jun via Getty Images; (l) Anadolu via Getty Images; p186 (bg) PA Images / Alamy Stock Photo; p187 (t) Everett Collection Inc / Alamy Stock Photo; (m) NGrey/Shutterstock; p188 (bg) Vasyl Shulga/Shutterstock; (r) ViDI Studio/Shutterstock; p189 (t) Associated Press / Alamy Stock Photo; (r) Morozova Olga/Shutterstock; pp190–191 (bg) irin-k /Shutterstock; (m) Master1305/Shutterstock; (bg) FamVeld/Shutterstock; p192 (m) wavebreakmedia/Shutterstock; (l) SpeedKingz/Shutterstock; p193 (bg) Carlos Caetano/Shutterstock; p194 (bg) Sergey Novikov/Shutterstock; p195 (bg) Monkey Business Images/Shutterstock; p196 (t) Eivaisla/Shutterstock; (bg) StockImageFactory.com/Shutterstock; p197 (bg) Monkey Business Images/Shutterstock; p198 MoMo Productions via Getty Images; p199 (l) Altitude Visual/Shutterstock; (m) Inside Creative House/Shutterstock; p201 (t) Dean Drobot/Shutterstock; (br) wavebreakmedia/Shutterstock; (l) oriori/Shutterstock; pp202–203 (bg) michaeljung/Shutterstock; pp204–205 (bg) AnnaStills/Shutterstock; pp206–207 (bg) Monkey Business Images/Shutterstock; p209 (bg) TierneyMJ/Shutterstock; (m) paulaphoto/Shutterstock; p210 Ray Bond/Shutterstock; p211 Andrey_Popov/Shutterstock; p212 (l) R-O-M-A/Shutterstock; (m) MyImages – Micha/Shutterstock; pp212–213 (bg) Andrew Angelov/Shutterstock; p213 (t) Montree sangpa/Shutterstock; (tr) Audrius Merfeldas/Shutterstock; (bl) Creatsy/Shutterstock; pp214–215 ConceptCafe/Shutterstock; pp216–217 (bg) doublelee/Shutterstock; p216 (m) ronstik/Shutterstock; (r) fatamorgana-999/Shutterstock; p217 (m) Sergiy Kuzmin/Shutterstock; (l) Carolyn Jenkins / Alamy Stock Photo; p218 (mr) Everett Collection Inc / Alamy Stock Photo; (br) Atibordee Kongprepan/Shutterstock; p219 Mike Coppola / Getty Images Entertainment via Getty Images; p220 (r) koya979/Shutterstock; (b) Majonit/Shutterstock; p221 (bg) Naoki Kim/Shutterstock; (r) Lukassek/Shutterstock; (b) Jam Press /@rfedortsov_official_account; p222 gd_project/Shutterstock; p223 (t) eyematter/Shutterstock; (b) object_photo/Shutterstock; p224 (bg) Gisele Yashar/Shutterstock; (tr) Proton-stock/Shutterstock; (t) TheFarAwayKingdom/Shutterstock; (tm) Sweatshirt BD Gallery/Shutterstock; (l) Iv-olga/Shutterstock; (rm) Ekaterina_Minaeva/Shutterstock; (m) Craig Russell/Shutterstock; (bm) Jarp2/Shutterstock; p225 Philip Scalia / Alamy Stock Photo; p226 (t) Olesia3/Shutterstock; (m) pukao/Shutterstock; (bl) Steve Mack / Alamy Stock Photo; p227 (t) Christian webster/Shutterstock; (b) 80's Child/Shutterstock; p228 (tl) NTU Singapore; (bl) Auctioneum Bristol & Bath; p229 Alexanderstock23/Shutterstock; p230 (l) Roman Samokhin/Shutterstock; (tr) P Maxwell Photography/Shutterstock; (br) Best_photo_studio/Shutterstock; p231 pauloalberto82/Shutterstock; p232 Johannes Kornelius/Shutterstock; p233 Roman Sigaev/Shutterstock; p234 Vitalii Hulai/Shutterstock; p235 Atibordee Kongprepan; p237 ifong/Shutterstock; p238 Mirelle/Shutterstock; back cover: (tr) RT Design Studio/Shutterstock; (bm) La Gorda/Shutterstock; (br) NikoNomad/Shutterstock; (ml) koya979/Shutterstock; (ml) Marti Bug Catcher/Shutterstock; (tl) irin-k/Shutterstock; (bl) Cornel Pop/Shutterstock.